At the Edge of Wonder:
Gazing into Mystery

by Jim Conlon

Planetary People Press
www.becomingplanetarypeople.com

Planetary People Press
An Imprint of JTT Marketing LLC
562 Winthrop Road
Union, NJ 07083

Please direct permissions requests to:
john@jttmarketing.com.

Printed in the United States of America

Conlon, Jim, 1936—

Wondering Between Two Worlds: Awakening to the Living God
Print ISBN: 978-0-578-40373-1

Praise for *At the Edge of Wonder*

Jim Conlon, as usual, gives us here much to think and pray about. His poetry and meditations keep us close to Earth, and in doing so, provide fresh and wide-open avenues to the encounter with God.

—John F. Haught, author *The New Cosmic Story: Inside Our Awakening Universe* (Yale Univ. Press, 2017)

At the Edge of Wonder offers the reader a poetic feast for the soul. A deep and expansive cache of wisdom. Gentle yet strong, both comforting and challenging. A book to awaken hope and strengthen action for good amid our troubled world.

—Joyce Rupp, author of numerous bestselling books, spiritual midwife, retreat leader

Jim Conlon has gifted us over the years with his deep sensitivity to the movements of divine love in the dynamic flow of life. In these beautiful poems and meditations, he leads us into the flow of divine creative love hovering on the edge of the soul, the edge of the heart, the edge of the universe. On the edge of chaos, life is born over and over again. This is the Good News: in a world that seems to be falling apart, living on the edge of chaos means living in the heart of divine love.

—Ilia Delio, OSF, Villanova University

Table of Contents

Dedication

I dedicate these pages to all my good companions who have joined me on the journey these many years. To all, I am very grateful.

Foreword

I am fascinated by the title of this book. It evokes several connections with what modern scientists call "the edge of chaos," which does not describe the onset of chaos but its after-effects. Chaos theory describes a state of internal dislocation, because the old certainties don't make sense anymore. The order begins to disintegrate, disorder ensues, and the system veers toward a freshly discovered sense of coherence.

This is the edge of chaos. The old will never be the same again, but the new is still unfolding—sometimes confusing, chaotic, stretching, even exciting. It is not neat and precise like the old order, but intuition tells us that it is a great deal more real, and this is what compels credibility.

Jim Conlon brings a creative and intuitive mind to the "edge of wonder"; he goes beyond wondering—as we saw in the first volume of this series, *Wondering Between Two Worlds*—into the realm of *wonder*. And this journey is no longer just personal, interpersonal, or social. It is planetary, global, and cosmic. This is Conlon's revolutionary insight. Moving through the four spheres of soul, life, Earth and the divine, the psychologist within me hears resonances of stages of developmental growth. The difference, of course, is that these are planetary/cosmic stages and not merely personal ones.

This is precisely what the edge of chaos is about. The previous, familiar world of conventional wisdom no longer holds. The certainties crumble, the clarity fades, the boundaries are stretched, often beyond recognition. We are into new territory: disturbing, dangerous, challenging, but for growing numbers among us, exciting and promising. Assuredly, we have been there before, and nobody knows the territory better than the mystics both ancient and recent. Jim Conlon graciously acknowledges their enduring contribution.

But even for the mystics there is a radical newness. We encounter a new evolutionary movement that is beginning to dawn upon our world. None of us has been there before. We need fresh wisdom for our time and for our journey. You would be advised to take along a copy of *At the Edge of Wonder*. You'll find it a useful resource, solace for the turbulent times, guidance at the crossroads, and above all reassurance for the different future that embraces our world in these opening decades of the 21st century.

—Diarmuid O'Murchu, June 2018

Introduction

As the world continues to churn with ripples of unrest, we pursue a new moment of solitude as we peer over the precipice of wonder and gaze into the mystery before us. Mystery envelops our awareness of society and soul and encompasses the sacred planet in this new moment of grace, as the divine presence continues to unfold. We allow our imagination to soar and to embrace the beauty of creation, even amidst the poverty and devastation that reside across the world these days.

We pray today that from the depths of our society, planet, and soul, we may be anointed with a healing bond of freedom that will touch the world with wonder, mystery, and surprise. Emerging from this new moment, we venture forth into each galactic opportunity to experience the depth of the incarnation, to wonder as "the flesh becomes word" and flares forth into an as-yet-unimagined life.

With each new awareness, we remember how life burst forth on this planet and gave birth to the untrodden path that it is now our challenge to walk. As we move toward accomplishing the next steps on our journey, we compose the beatitudes of the new creation that dares to await us and calls us forth into an era of grateful peace.

We hear the call today. It is a cry for fresh energy and zest for life, in a moment of aliveness and a moment of grace. As we cocreate a wondrous future to heal the Earth and nourish new life, we listen attentively with gratitude and joy to the longings of creation. We venture forth into a time of prolonged engagement, when our dreams will emerge from the deep wells of wisdom. We imagine a new era that will refresh our souls and renew the face of the Earth.

As beauty bursts forth, we feel the joyful and tender embrace of soul, life, and Earth, enveloped in the sacred, pulsating presence of our God. This presence will heal all our longings and quench our thirst for sacredness. As we announce the great "I am" of the gospel that pulsates through each of our days, we long to tell the story of how things began. The sacred breakthrough moments of creation, liberation, and contemplation bubble up from our hearts and invite us toward fresh engagement. On our journey, the Spirit speaks to us at the edge of wonder as we gaze into the mystery of our emerging, viable, and energized future.

Silent Depths

Allow your heart to swell,
mind to open,
soul to grow.

Ponder the face of Jesus,
listen to Pope Francis,
discover God
in our flawed and fractured world.

Follow the promptings of the spirit
in the midst of each new moment,
experience the fireball in your heart.
From silent depths of wonder,
let flow the energy of love.

The Wonder of Mystery

I arise today
from the clouds
of forgetfulness
and recent sleep,
liberated from the cell blocks
of past sorrow and regret.

I arise today
within the healing balm
of chrism
that trickles
across my wounded soul.

"Stay the course of courage,"
I hear wisdom say.
"Embrace fresh freedom,
remember those
who have gone before."

I welcome mercy,
anticipate the morning,
stay awake and wonder
about mystery and soul.

AT THE EDGE OF SOUL

Jim Conlon

A Canticle to Soul

Let us give voice to our unspoken hunger,
to our quest for sacredness and depth.

Let us keep on believing
in the fruitfulness of our efforts.

Let us join with those who are willing
to risk their lives and lifestyles
that others may flourish and live.

Let us become sensitive
to the poverty of the planet
and listen to people in pain.

Let us nurture new expressions of compassion
and co-create structures of peace.

Let us become fully present
to those we love.

Let us nurture a new spirituality
to energize a world of harmony, balance and peace.

Let us celebrate Earth as a living community
and our common home.

Let us practice nonviolence
and celebrate each moment
as an epiphany of kindness, beauty, listening and love.

Let us remember our story
and let go of anything that stands in the way
of living fully with a listening heart.

Let us search for the subtle presence of the divine,
especially in the cry of the poor, who allow the divine to
shine through.

Let us search for sacredness and depth,
where the unspoken hunger reveals
the language of connectedness, spirit and soul.

And we will discover who we really are.

Contemplation and Soul

Soul happens in relationship, in moments of intimacy and of solitude. As we remember incidents of depth, experiences touch the heart, and our spirit soars. We imagine healing all separateness and are embraced in the genuine depths of compassion, home, silence, friendship, and inclusion. Soul becomes a compass of hope.

Thomas Berry says, "Soul is fundamentally a biological concept, defined as the primary organizing, sustaining, and guiding principle of a living being.... The universe and the human soul find their fulfillment in each other. Soul gives to the multitude of living forms wondrous powers of movement and reproduction, but even more wondrous powers of sensation and emotion.... The entire universe is shaped and sustained in all its interwoven patterns by the mysterious powers of soul."

The longing of soul can be best understood through the lens of contemplative theology. Here we focus our conscious attention on the presence of the divine in all things; as we respond to the longing of the soul, we integrate our experience through a deeper awareness of the interior life and the mystery of existence.

In contemplation, we commune with cosmic forces, with ultimate mystery. We practice a spirituality born out of the depths of the universe in moments of intimacy and solitude.

God Is Alive Within

God's presence is alive within;
even in the leaf, God is there.
There are so many mysteries.
The tiniest little creatures of nature
teach us all to be grandmothers and grandfathers.
Everything is relationship and holy awe.

A Sabbath for the Soul

Our souls are shaped by stories: the stories we hear and stories we tell ourselves. Those narratives give shape to who we are in our own eyes. They also name the sequence of events that tell others about us, and identify who we are to the world.

A primary threshold to freedom is telling our story differently—to include our accomplishments and also to emerge from the closet of self-deprecation, to transform a self-taught litany of failure into a banquet of blessings, to announce our presence as an unexpected moment when grace entered our lives and provided in the midst of turbulence a Sabbath for the soul.

Moments of Sabbath and rest happen when the longing of the soul is quenched, and we are one with our heart's pursuit. These mystical moments heal the heart and envelop us in a mystery that alters and illuminates our lives.

I recall many such moments:

In the backyard with my baseball coach as I listened eagerly to his reflections on the game of life.

Witnessing the beauty of the stars, the trajectory of a swallow in flight, the arching leap of a pickerel from silken waters as the sun recedes in the West.

Moments of portent and prophecy while following in the footsteps of Dr. Martin Luther King, Jr., on Woodward Avenue in Detroit, Michigan, as my heart opened and my imagination soared to embrace the social gospel as a vehicle to alter and illuminate our lives.

Moments when, after years of study and reflection, mystical and engaged spirituality became more than words.

Moments when suddenly, as if for the first time, I became one with the star, the sunset, the bird, the fish, the mentor, and saw in each the God who came down from heaven.

Each moment, a Sabbath for the soul.

Stories

I ask the swallow
singing in the meadow,
"What shall I say?"
Swallow answers,
"Tell them the story."

I ask the deer
frolicking in the field,
"What shall I say?"
Deer calls back,
"Tell them the story."

I ask the ancestors
gathered around,
"What shall I say?"
They answer back,
"Remember to tell our story.
Tell the story of every being,
from the birth of the universe
until now, and everything in between."

Stories of courage.
Stories of beauty
and overflowing love.
Stories of wonder and surprise.
Stories of wisdom.
Stories from the heart
that were told before
yet are forever new.

Balm for the Soul

Deep within the restless world
resides a profound pursuit,
an uncommon quest
for intimacy and rest,
a longing for peace,
for relief on the journey,
for a loving embrace
that heals the heart,
that is balm for the soul,
that longs to just be.

Grace Happens

Grace happens when we explore the deep inner currents of belonging and realize the profound connection between our aspirations for life and the concrete requirements for living.

Grace happens in possible and sometimes impossible ways.

Grace happens when our mood shifts, and we discover new people and projects in seemingly mysterious ways.

Grace happens when we discover anew that life has its own trajectory and that we know deeply that we live in a universe where we are not in charge.

Grace happens when we discover that life requires effort, often in what feels like effortless ways.

Grace happens when we work hard and stay focused, yet realize the outcomes are far beyond our awareness, energies, or control.

Grace happens as a gift, a manifestation of an unfolding universe whose ultimate trajectory is always toward the good.

Grace happens when life becomes embedded in mystery and surprise.

Grace happens when we awaken to many questions and are willing to remain uncertain, yet in pursuit of the quest.

Grace happens when, in our soul searching, we find a way to heal the wounds of childhood.

Grace happens when science speaks to us and reveals its many patterns on our path.

Grace happens when, in the midst of our search, we discover that place of hope where our secret longings lie.

Grace happens when, in our restlessness, we discover colleagues in pursuit of justice who also long for a life of harmony, balance, and peace.

Grace happens when we discover at the threshold of unexplored frontiers a quantum realm wherein reside the secrets of what it means to be alive.

Grace happens when we embark anew on a journey to celebrate fresh expressions of wisdom, to see each expression of creation as a unique manifestation of sacredness and new life.

Dinner with Donna at Christmas

It was Christmas morning in Brielle, New Jersey. Outside, the winds sent blistering sheets of rain across the windows and into the streets. Snow was promised by the forecasters as people in this village on the Jersey Shore and other coast-side towns prepared to stay inside, away from winter's fury on this day on which we celebrate a child's birth.

The doorbell rang. My sister and I welcomed my sister's friend Fran and her friend Donna to our newly formed Christmas Day community. Fran was a volunteer with the Arc, an organization serving people with intellectual and developmental disabilities, and had chosen to share the holiday with Donna, a developmentally challenged adult, and with us.

Donna's presence among us turned out to be a gift, an unexpected incarnation on that nativity morning, encouraging us to reflect in a new way on the meaning of the day and what it is that we, in fact, celebrate on Christmas.

As I entered into Donna's obvious enjoyment of her Christmas lunch, I found myself musing on Christmas and its meaning for Donna, myself, and others in the twenty-first century. I understood the incarnation as the interface between divinity and creation, spirit and matter, humanity and the other-than-human world.

On that Christmas day, as the rain turned to snow, the meal was complete. In the companionable silence that followed, I heard whispers about the birth of newness. Once again incarnation happened, divinity was present, and the Earth community vibrated with new life. Donna gathered her presents of clothes, candy, and cards, and with happy smiles took her leave to be driven home by Fran. As they vanished into the night, I was conscious of my own wounds and weaknesses, sometimes more hidden than our guest's. The meaning of Christmas seemed clearer. Divinity had visited us in the person of a woman, Donna, whose very wounds and uncomplicated wisdom were the manger of newness on that Incarnation Day.

A Mysterious Invitation

A mysterious call
echoes in your heart,
calls you forward
into an unplanned life.

In this a moment,
you are called to shake off
the inertia of life,
to awaken to new awareness.

Now is the time
to embark on untrodden paths.
Find a life aligned with purpose,
activate the summons
woven deeply into your soul.

This time of transition
calls you to return
to your early years.
With a beginners' mind,
celebrate all that is promising and free.

Today embrace gratefully
what is still possible for you to do.
Through recollections,
struggle and fulfillment,
look back and begin again.

The Search

Diving deep into the cosmic water of uncertainty,
new frontiers of exploration beckon me.
Magnetic intuition draws me forth
into a gravitational adventure of the soul.

Newfound engagement stirs deeply;
in the uncertainty of the moment,
a shattering occurs.
As once, as if forever and yet for the first time,
a cosmic vista emerges and unfolds.

Incarnation happens
at the epicenter of my soul
as I begin to understand
at least for now and maybe later
that I am a child of the universe,
a child longing for wisdom
and searching for home.

I long to discover relatedness
and the deep nurturing mystery
that is the resource for connectedness
and the resonating fire of my soul.

And so I wander forth in search of
meaning, purpose, passion and life.
I wander forth in search of
wonder and surprise.
I wander forth in search of

balance, wisdom and a listening heart.
I wander forth in search of
my place in an unfolding universe.

I wander forth in search of
a newfound strength to struggle
and discover within the recesses of my soul
the wellspring I dare to call my life.

I wander forth in careless abandon,
always giving notice
that my place in the universe
is contained in the seeds
of all that I am, have been and will become.

Those geological events
that formed our planet
now are the basis of our being.
Those incidents of new life
that spring forth from the sea
flourish now on the hillside of our home.

All that has lead up to this galactic moment
of wisdom and surprise
cascaded into consciousness
and culminated in the person that is me.

And so the journey continues,
wrapped in an envelope of uncertainty,
embracing both hope and terror,
with a newfound vision of tomorrow
and a peace that may never cease.

Bethlehem Needs to Happen

Bethlehem needs to happen:

Through the welcoming of world religions into a unity of planetary peace.

In the celebration of science, art, and mysticism, to recover a new origin story for our lives.

Through radical listening and storytelling, so that we may come home to the rich soil of our psyches.

So that we may recover the wisdom of a theology of the incarnation, and find in the differentiated unity of the Trinity, a basis for reverence and love.

So that we may find in the liberating practices of cultural work, primary actions for freedom and geo-justice making.

In places of worship, so that healing can come to our bodies, to our imaginations, and to our authentic desire to create, through the arts and the art of prayer, the art of our lives.

In hospital emergency rooms and outpatient clinics, so welcoming can happen and compassion can be born.

In school classrooms so that feelings, intuitions, and ideas can commune, without the fear of guns and violence.

So that capitalism can be healed of its competition, and social policy can recover a sensitivity to spirit.

So that acquisitiveness and lifestyles of apparent necessity can give way to simplicity and a reverential use of energy.

So that gatherings and communities can respect differences, while individuals and outsiders are welcomed into the fabric of support and solution.

So that spring can continually be born of winter.

So that the seasons of the Earth can also be the seasons of our heart.

So that we may reverence creation for its own sake.

So that fields of plenty grow bread for a hungry world.

Where waters are poisoned, the Earth is pummeled with fertilizers, and the air is clogged with pollution.

When the aspirations of youth are crushed by cynicism, and the wisdom of age is discarded and repressed.

So that we can see in the incarnation of Christmas an event that continues today; a genesis that continues to happen in our cosmos, in our psyches, and in our souls.

So that an incarnation story of our time can emerge from the heart of oneness.

Pulse

Pulsating and listening,
breathing in and breathing out,
the energy of life
flows into every corner of existence.
The breath of life
streams into every soul,
make us one again,
one with the flowers,
one with the rain,
one with spirit,
one with pain.
Breath make us one body.
One spirit calls us by our name.

Celebrate

Pay homage to origins.
Honor the cosmic womb.
Be grateful for beauty.
Remember your story.

Pay attention to this moment.
Listen to your heart.
Rediscover hope.
Become what you were meant to be.

Within this arch of wisdom,
relationships extend
energizing commitment to a hope-filled life,
transcending all despair.

Embrace the crucible.
Welcome the primordial furnace.
Notice moments of the unexpected,
each an opportunity to celebrate,
celebrate,
celebrate.

Jim Conlon

Freshness

Nourish the spirit.
Celebrate the energy of life.
Welcome the triune one.
Greet each new moment.
Become an integral presence,
a felt sense of the sacred,
Everything belongs,
as from turbulence,
an ordered future flows.

Reflections at the Edge of Soul

The spiritual journey contains a variety of ingredients: courage, openness, compassion, integral consciousness, and love. This is the expression of a generous and abundant universe.

Through mystical engagement, we contemplate the depths of the psyche and receive images, symbols, and archetypes from the wellspring of our soul.

As we bring to conscious expression what lies in the recesses of our psyches, we fashion a holistic spirituality that is aligned to the cosmos, resides within the soul, and culminates in a compassionate commitment to the prophetic struggle.

Jim Conlon

Sacred Seekers

May we sacred seekers
venture forth
to compose a new chapter
in the great story,
nourished by the friendship
of good companions
on our unfinished journey.

The Soul's Journey into Sacredness: Ten Spiritual Practices

There are ten spiritual practices I'd like to highlight that contribute to our journey into sacredness and depth. They are listening, heeding the prophets, letting go, storytelling, exercising compassion, celebrating creativity, spending time with the little ones, honoring the beauty of creation, making authentic rituals, and harboring hope and vision.

Listening is the capacity not just to hear with our ears but to be open to whatever and wherever the universe chooses to communicate with us. It could be from a bird, a breeze, or a tree; or in the prophetic voice of a Dr. Martin Luther King, Jr., or a Mahatma Gandhi; or in the canonical texts of our traditions, whether the Hebrew or Christian Bible, the Qur'an, or ancestral voices. Such a listening heart also enables us to attend to the promptings of our own souls. Intuition, the capacity to be open to what some call "that still small voice" is an expression of such listening.

Part of listening is giving recognition to another. Listening is not about giving advice. When others talk about their lives, you don't need to have answers for them. They aren't really looking for answers from you. They just want someone to listen. Most of us have our own answers; we long for an opportunity to access the clarity that exists deep within us. That clarity comes through being listened to and being able to listen to ourselves. Recognition provides the attention that makes the listening possible. It's both a great challenge and also a priceless gift just to listen.

One definition for *spirituality* is the capacity for a listening heart. The listening heart is sensitive and receptive to all the interactions and relationships we either endure or celebrate. We listen with the ears of the soul. Listening and recognition are at the center of the spiritual life and are a profound way to grow our soul. Brother David Steindl-Rast, OSB, says that a listening heart involves the experience of faith, hope, and love through existential trust, openness to surprise, and saying yes to belonging.

Listening and recognition are the greatest gifts we can give to another and also to ourselves. Their practice invites intimacy; makes communication possible; energizes the spirit; and creates a context, a fertile silence, to foster wisdom. To listen is a permanent attitude of being open to the word of the other, to the gesture of the other, to the difference of the other. Listening requires a generous and loving heart, respect, tolerance, humility, joy, love. It requires openness to what is new, to what is welcome, to change, to perseverance, to struggle, to hope, and to justice. Listening gives access to what is eternally true, to the heart of wisdom, of liberation, of creation. It flows from a conviction that life is ours to create. By listening, we can satisfy the longing for intimacy, the cravings of our soul for life.

One of the first steps in the creative process is learning to be silent. Learning to live with silence. Wisdom is the capacity for a listening heart. Through a listening heart, we are tuned in and attuned to the voice within and the voice without. Stories are based on listening and recognition. There is no story if nobody listens. There is no story if there is no one to tell it. Silence is the birthplace of creativity. It also gives us the capacity to move beyond illusion to reality.

Heeding the prophets is another way to grow our soul. It is important to understand that neither the prophets of the Old Testament (e.g., Daniel and Samuel and Isaiah) nor the prophets of our time (e.g., King, Gandhi, Dorothy Day, Cesar Chavez, Bede Griffith, Thomas Merton, and perhaps your own ancestors) are asking us to imitate them. They are asking us to be inspired by our own vision and energized by their words, so we can find our own way. What matters is our own response to this prophetic moment, be it in the church, in the workplace, in the family, or in the society that truly needs our help.

Rabbi Heschel, the great Jewish mystic, wrote, "There's a grain of the prophet in the recesses of every human soul." It is such a vision that calls upon us to be a people of protest and prophecy, to stand on our principles, to speak truth to power, and to dare to tell the truth.

Today, prophets are being recognized as they confront the issues of environmental devastation, climate change, and social justice, among others. John

Seed and Joanna Macy envisioned a Council of All Beings where humans stand in the center and all the other species have a chance to talk to the humans about how they have mistreated the planet: "I don't like what you're doing to my water" or "Why did you cut down my trees?" Then the humans come to the outside and apologize to all the other species, who are now in the center. A Council of All Beings is a kind of "ecozoic council," to use Thomas Berry's phrase. It supports and energizes the prophetic groups that have sprung up all over the country and all over the world. We need to lend our voices to making the planet a mutually enriching place to live, not just for us but for the children of the next generation and beyond.

Letting go is a practice that exists within almost every tradition, even if different language is used to describe it. Buddhism talks about the dangers of attachment, which can also be described as clinging. It's the clinging, not the object of the attachment, that is the problem. One of the reasons we have a pathological culture is our collective inability to let go.

Culture is made up of many elements that differ from people to people: different stories; different music; different ancestral myths; different creation stories; different art forms; different rituals; different values; different media, ethics and customs. Our spirituality is intimately connected to all these cultural elements. It's embodied. It's contextualized. If we judge some elements of our culture to be pathological, we need to seek a spiritual practice that will allow us to engage in cultural therapy to heal the illness we experience. One such practice is the process of letting go.

In the life of the medieval mystic John of the Cross, we find a powerful example of the practice of letting go. He suffered abuse, pain, and incarceration, but he did not hold onto anger, bitterness, or despair. John of the Cross wrote about what he called "the dark night of the soul." Some would describe the dark night as the experience of falling out of a plane and discovering your parachute won't open. We're living today in the dark night of our cultural soul, as well as of our personal experiences. We need to learn to break through our fear and let go of the unnecessary limitations we place on our envisioning of what life can be.

The process of letting go is catalyzed by events in our lives. It is a spiritual strategy for dealing with pain, disappointment, and all of the bitter and burdensome events that are part and parcel of our lives. The opposite of letting go is thinking that we have all the answers, that we have a predetermined plan for our lives, that we've got it all figured out ahead of time. Letting go means that the creative energy of the divine is allowed expression within and through us. It's like being on a sailboat when the wind comes up, and allowing it to take the boat on a new course. That wind takes you to a place you could never have discovered on your own. When our mental categories shatter in such a way, we can feel the turbulence inside. The way we saw the world is challenged and reorganized.

Another dimension of the letting go process is coming to terms with the fact that we are divine. Letting go means moving from culture of narcissism to a culture of mysticism. Narcissism means we're centered on ourselves through inordinate psychic introspection. Everything is us. The world circles around us. Mysticism is cosmically centered: it is a oneness with all that is.

Part of the process of letting go is forgiving ourselves, acknowledging our original goodness, and realizing that we are still inherently good. Letting go is also about forgiving others. Forgiving those who have offended us is letting go of the enemy.

And what about letting go of a dull life or one lived only in memory? Norman Cousins says, "The tragedy of life is not death, but what we let die inside while we are still alive." John O'Donohue says, "One of the greatest sins is the unlived life." I had a friend who was a hospice nurse. When she talked to her patients, many of whom had cancer, she would ask, "How has cancer blessed your life?" The stories of gratitude she heard were amazing. On a deep level, we know that whatever happens rebounds with good.

Think of your own stories of grief and loss and letting go—whether with a spouse, a relationship, an occupation, or an illness. At one moment, it feels devastating, and it is, but ultimately something new shines through. The act of surrender and letting go is part of the human journey. Meister Eckhart says it this way: "God is not found in the soul by adding anything but by a process of subtraction."

When I was a little boy in Ontario, we had a pear tree in the backyard. My father would prune it, and after he cut some of the branches off, the poor thing looked rather withered and unspectacular. But then the next year, guess what? Bigger pears! Juicier pears. We grow our soul just like that pear tree. When things somehow are, or appear to be, taken from us, it creates the opportunity for something new to come through. It is a great paradox, but it is profound and always present. The soul grows by subtraction.

Storytelling is at the center of the spiritual journey. Jack Shea is a great storyteller. He wrote *Stories of God, Stories of Faith*, and *Gospel Light*. He says if you feel consoled, inspired, and healed by stories, it's because they've connected you with the loving vitality of soul. Therefore, one way to grow your soul is to tell your story. Reflect on your story. Gather in groups, or wisdom circles, to tell the stories of your ancestors, of your grandkids, of your children, of your communities, of your tradition, of the universe. Tell the stories of all those things you hold dear.

Every tradition uses stories as a vehicle for communication. We tell stories as a way of identifying who we are. Our culture also has stories, as does our universe. Our lives can be viewed from these three perspectives: the personal, the cultural, and the cosmic. The stories we're writing about ourselves and the story of society and the story of the universe are all one story. One of the major insights of our time is that our lives are chapters in the bigger story.

Classic psychotherapy is storytelling. Therapy is changing our personal story from woundology to original goodness. That's the process of healing. We locate our story within the larger universe. A story energizes us. There's something about being able to tell our story that heals us, that makes pain more bearable.

When you get to know somebody, you want to hear his or her story. You want to know where that person came from, what his or her origins are. From that, you might have some idea where the person is at this moment and who he or she is, and gain a glimpse of the future.

The spiritual practice of storytelling is the practice of remembering. You can't tell a story without a memory. Stories reveal changes and transformational moments. The shifts that happen over time are incorporated into our stories. Self-reflective consciousness is the unique gift of humanity. We are the universe reflecting on itself. When we tell our stories, we are also speaking on behalf of the Earth.

Richard Harmon of the Industrial Areas Foundation NW Regional Office in Portland, Oregon, says, "When we speak from the center of our sacredness, the Earth in its pain and tenderness is speaking through us." Stories are a way that we achieve meaning. Patricia Mische, cofounder of Global Education Associates and professor of peace studies, says, "Stories are like membranes—they connect the world of our lives to the world out there." They're semipermeable membranes. Helen Prejean, author of *Dead Man Walking*, says, "There's no truth, only stories." When we tell stories and see the universe as a story, we're remembering the series of transformational events that appear over time, out of which this present moment evolves.

When we tell someone our story, we speak of defining moments. Thomas Berry would call them "moments of grace," those gifts of opportunity in which transformation is possible. Story is a way to access and express those moments of transformation. A story also knits together our inner fragmentation and then connects us to others so that we don't feel alone.

The story of the universe can be understood in four chapters: the galactic period from the flaring forth and formation of the elements; the formation of the Earth itself; the beginning-of-life period, when plants and animals emerged; and our chapter, the human period, marked by the rise of culture and consciousness. Though in our culture we tend to think of story as something written down in a book, something communicated exclusively with words, the stories we're talking about are broader than that. The birds tell a story, the sun tells a story, the breeze tells a story. Stories are communicated on many levels: sound and smell and image and light and darkness.

Every story is revelation. The divine is communicated to us through story. Our culture tends to have a

narrow vision of revelation, to confine it to the ca-
nonical scriptures and the time before the death of
the last apostle; thus, revelation is boxed in. In the
cosmological view, revelation happens daily, moment
by moment. It's happening right now. It's always un-
folding. The implications of that story are that every-
thing is valuable, that all dimensions of life should be
represented in any decision-making process, that the
divine is present everywhere, that diversity is some-
thing to celebrate and not repress.

Practicing compassion means being in an equal
relationship with those in need, whether human or
other-than-human. Compassion is not doing some-
thing for someone in a way that makes that person
feel inferior. Meister Eckhart says, 'The soul is where
God works compassion.' We grow our soul by the
practice of compassion.

Eckhart also says the best name for God is compas-
sion. My image of compassion is that of a mother
embracing her child—holding the child close, while
being willing to let go when the time comes. This
reminds me of the divine embrace of the universe,
which I see as a curvature of compassion. We live in
the arms of a universe where there is a balance be-
tween the forces of expansion and gravity. If either el-
ement were to get out of balance, our universe would
not exist.

This key reality of our universe—that our life de-
pends on achieving equilibrium—is reflected in
many aspects of human life, such as our striving to

balance our need for both continuity and discontinuity, or for innovation and tradition, in healthy ways. We need continuity with our roots, but we also need to live in this moment, making the tradition present and palpable today. Reflecting on the image of the divine curvature of compassion will give us insight and strength as we work to change the structures and worldview that have become desacralized.

Finding the compassionate curve that results from embracing each other, while mining the gold underneath the crust of our traditions, is what nurtures our lives. Imagine a volcano like the ones in Hawaii. When it is erupting, everything's fluid and warm and moving. After a while, however, the flow turns to rock, becomes rigid and stuck. We need theological air hammers to release the molten places underneath that crust of tradition so we can uncover the prophetic voice that is still fluid, the voice of compassion. In hope, commitment, community, celebration, creativity, transcendence, and compassion we experience the life of our tradition.

Celebrating creativity and imagination is at the heart of being fully human. Eckhart says, "If your heart is troubled, you're not yet a mother, you're still on the way to giving birth." What he meant by that is that there is a sense of dis-ease if we're not being creative, a feeling that something isn't right with us. Creativity is not dualistic. It's not objectifying. It is a mystical experience of being one with the clay, the painting, or the dance. There's an art gallery in Kleinburg, just north of Toronto, that houses the work of the Group of Seven. One of these Canadian artists, Lawren Harris, painted mountains and seascapes. Somebody asked him one time, "Lawren, what does it mean for you to be creative?" He said, "When I paint, I try to get to the summit of my soul, and I paint from there, where the universe sings."

Spending time with the little ones is another practice. Meister Eckhart wrote, "If I was really frightened, I would like to have a child with me, and if there were no children around, I would like an animal." Somehow the image of the divine is often revealed to us more clearly through the unprotected and the un-powerful.

This reminds me of Mark, a wonderful young man I met who seemed to radiate goodness. His mother told me that when he was applying for admission to a graduate program, he wrote the mandatory essay, which was a major part of determining whether he'd be accepted, about his dog, Maxie. The essay could have been a daunting task, but Mark took his dog with him and did just fine. His story suggests to me that being close to a little one, whether a child or an animal, is a way of accessing our connection to God. It's a way to deal with our fears. It's a way to grow our soul.

Honoring the beauty of creation is to have a sacramental consciousness by which we recognize the face of God in all of nature. This is another kind of literacy that all of us are capable of, though sometimes not conscious of, when we read God's face in a sunrise or sunset, a bluebonnet flower, a storm, a mountain range, a prairie, an ocean. These are the moments when creation speaks to us and tells us the story of the universe.

Jim Couture, a former student of mine, wrote, "The cavity of our souls needs to be filled with the wonder and awe of the natural world." We grow our soul every time we respond to such beauty.

Making authentic rituals is to speak the language of the soul. Why do we have ritual? Because we need symbolic language to express the deeper recesses of our hearts and minds and souls, to connect the conscious to the unconscious. There are cultural rituals, inspired by a spiritual impulse, such as processions for peace or protest. Prayer is a form of ritual. Rabbi Heschel says, "Prayer is meaningless unless it is subversive."

Eucharists don't only happen in churches. One Holy Thursday, I was privileged to be with a group of people in San Francisco who practice the gospel mandate of Jesus to wash the feet of the poor. We went around in groups and massaged the feet of the homeless as a gesture of service. Instead of actually washing their feet, we presented them with a pair of clean white socks. It was incredibly joyful.

Touching these people's feet often turned on fifty years of story. It just poured out of them. One woman said her marriage was broken, and she hadn't seen her family for years. She had written to all her granddaughters in Massachusetts, but only one had answered her. She went upstairs to the little room she lives in and brought down the letter to show me. It said, "Dear Grandma, I have your picture on my desk and when I do my homework, I look at you and I love you." That meant a lot to the woman. In this ritual, we both grew our souls, and I believe that act of service was Eucharist. Together we reenacted the Last Supper. Communion was happening.

Harboring hope and vision is essential to grow our soul. We need to have a vision and a dream of what our life could be. There's nothing sadder than a life spent just going through the motions. A lot of people are going through the motions, just hanging in there, always waiting, never taking initiative. For them, life has no deep meaning. We all need a vision and a dream to keep hope alive and to lead us to ask and seek an answer for Mary Oliver's question: "What is it you plan to do with your one wild and precious life?"

It takes a vision and a dream to draw you forward, to help you attend to that still small voice within, to the synchronicities of events; to discern your truth in what you hear from the pulpit, from your colleagues, from your spouse, from your children, from your puppy. At some moment, the shape of your future will become clearer and you will identify and claim the visions that were yours when you were born. Yours will not be an unlived life.

We can also grow our soul to recognize and respect

the sacredness and depth in what might seem to be unlikely places. A group called the Community Action Network in Dublin, Ireland, works with people who are homeless and who suffer from domestic violence, addiction, or unemployment, and other forms of human pathos that are so prevalent. When they get together, they ask people to go out and walk in the streets of the city. They have one requirement—that you walk with your "soul eyes" open. Soul eyes allow participants to see the sacredness and depth in all they encounter on their walk. When the members of this group return, they report seeing syringes on the street, a flower bursting forth in a garden, a homeless person, a child, the rain—everything with new compassion and clarity.

Where the Heart Is

A delicate place,
sprinkled with pictures,
artifacts, each holding a memory
of days long past,
each a welcome sign
for rest, creativity
and compassion.

Wherever you are,
no matter how lonely,
no matter how lost,
there is tender place of welcome,
a place to stir
the fetal waters of your soul,
that you may rest
and bring to birth new things
on this heart-felt day.

Heart's Journey

Listen to the rain,
the clouds at night,
sunburst mornings,
amidst a silent cry.

Become a scribe today.
The inscriptions on your heart
have many tales to tell
about what echoes in the night.

Listen deeply
to the unspoken wisdom
flowing through the currents of life.
Become alive and listen.

Respond to the promptings.
Venture forth to the unknown place
where wisdom lies.
Discover there the journey of your heart.

Soul Work

Soul work moves us from illusion to reality. It is less about petition and contrition than about attuning our lives and minds to the unfolding dynamics of the universe.

Soul work is an encounter with beauty and pain, an expression of gratitude and a search for meaning, a language that transcends all traditions.

In spiritual practice, we become a poet and a politician.

In soul work, we contact the pulsating, originating energy of the universe. Through receptivity and response, we experience what we long for. We dive deeply into the joys and sorrows of life and experience the solidarity of engagement.

Soul work and spiritual practice are an attitude of the heart, an openness to the meaning of existence. Through soul work, we gain perspective on God's action in the world.

In our spiritual practice, we realize that challenge, fear, gratitude, hope for possibilities, and tendencies toward self-destruction are present in all people. We discover that life's mysteries are present in everyone.

Sound spiritual practice is dialectical (e.g., progressive and conservative, innovative and traditional).

Our soul work includes silent recollection and engaged action, a vulnerability to wonder, an invitation to mystery, an openness to reverence, an experience of belonging, and an awareness of the sacredness of life.

Soul work names and celebrates the dramatic moments of creativity and new life, We name the human journey within the context of the Paschal mystery, and we intensify the mystery in everyday existence. We become continuously reminded that tomorrow can be different from today, that our deepest longings have a cosmic and sacred source.

Prayer happens through our interaction with others. It is here that we discover who we are. It is here that revelation happens. Through our engagements, we choose again and again the path to transformation and discover that true life on Earth is possible.

Soul work happens in stillness. In transparent moments, we perceive the universe. We experience gratitude and joy, validity and purpose, and become energized for the journey toward meaning and fulfillment.

Jim Conlon

Out of the Dark

In the dark, I wander,
searching in the night
for signs of wonder
in the mystery
I dare to call my life.

Now is the time,
when the thick haze
of uncertainty and doubt,
awaken for one brief
unseen moment.

The fog is lifted now,
clarity appears,
with one more
wondering step
into a shared horizon.

My sacred quest,
where often all seemed lost,
vanished, and appeared again
in this timeless moment.
My quest, revealed your face!

Artists of Life

When evolutionary philosopher Brian Swimme was writing *The Hidden Heart of the Cosmos*, his working title was *The All-Nourishing Abyss*. He meant that nothingness is the source of life, ideas, the universe, and creativity. The original fireball, that creative moment that marks the beginning of the universe, cannot be calculated from its very beginning point. There is a time, a mysterious moment, that people of faith call the divine creative act. Out of nothingness, in a sense, everything is born.

It's my conviction that the most profound impulse, the most sacred longing of soul that any of us has, is to understand and express our creativity.

Creativity is the impulse inside us that has to find expression. It will do so either in a benevolent way or in a destructive way. Much of the violence in our culture is repressed creativity, as is much of the burnout in our workaday world. Institutional structures are afraid of change and therefore do not encourage creativity.

Creativity, however, is not just one option among many. It's a precondition for an authentic life. Many people spend the first half of their lives enjoying things and then the second half of their lives discovering who they are. The problem with such self-discovery occurs when we rely on psychological techniques to tell us who we are. "I'm a 6." "I'm an INFP." "I'm an obsessive-compulsive." I don't think psychological techniques reveal the authentic self. I'm not saying that enneagrams and Myers-Briggs and other psychological tools aren't valid, but that they don't really get to the core of who we are. The way we discover ourselves is through the creative act, not through psychological techniques.

The artist always leads. The imagination precedes the intellect, always. Using our imaginations, allowing our creative hearts to express themselves in all areas of our lives, grows our souls.

Creativity takes courage. Anastasia MacDonald, a former student of mine, coined a word: *creageous*. She combined *courage and creativity* into one word. The prophets of today are people of courage and creativity. They are the saints of tomorrow and are often exiled in their own time. Anastasia wrote a poem expanding on the word's definition:

Deciding without knowing where it will take me,
Returning to my easel when the paints made me cry last
    week,
Dancing no matter who is watching,
Writing when there is no language to express my
    experience,
Being silent and listening,
Pursuing subjects that make me nervous,
Singing to hear my voice,
Raising my hand and saying, "I will,"
Asking for dreams night after night,

Creageous is stepping off looking up not down.

We are never more like God than when we are creating. Each individual is unique, a reflection of the divine, and our acts of creation enhance the likeness. Freud said of his work, "Everywhere I go, I find a poet has been there before me." A scientist I know in British Columbia was working on a complicated theorem. One creative person took a look at the problem and gave him the answer, but it was ten years before they worked out the equations.

The creative process is the doorway into the new story. One can't be a machine, or think like one, and be creative. The two are incompatible. The creative process is about unleashing the imagination and entering into the spirit of mysticism, which can be understood as the resurrection of our soul. It is the consciousness of a new worldview. In our deepest self, we are at one with the universe, with ourselves, with one another, with creation, and with the divine.

Standing in downtown Louisville, Thomas Merton suddenly said, "I love everybody! I am awakening from the dream of separateness." That's what creativity does for us. It awakens us from the dream of separateness—from the nightmare of gun violence, the despair of youth, old people stuck in filing cabinets called retirement communities, the distance and alienation from the very source of our own life and being.

The creative process requires a movement from illusion

to reality. What blocks us are our misconceptions about who we are or what it is we are called to create. Spiritual practices, such as meditation, ritual, movement, journaling, and conversations with a friend, stimulate creativity. All of these deepen the process and unleash the imagination. Retreat or sabbatical time—whether a year away to study; a couple of hours in the park; or time for a walk with a child, friend, or puppy—is also necessary. At its deepest level, time away reminds us that the world will survive without us. Things will go on. Retreat time means being able to live without doing something. It means rest, leisure, a time to catch our breath. Often our best ideas occur when we're not trying to solve a problem. When we want to grind away at an idea but instead go for a walk, all of a sudden, the very things we were trying to deal with fall into place. Retreat time is a source of the creative process.

Through creativity, we confront our mortality. We experience resurrection and make it possible for the result of our creative act to live on beyond us—be it as a child, poem, project, or idea.

I think we should take a vow of creativity, a vow to allow our imaginations to act in ways we have not planned. The creative process is like parenting a child: first you give it life, then you give it love, and then you let it go. One of the reasons creativity is so challenging for us is that we want to control what we create. Parents know that is impossible. The same is true of a relationship. It is also true of a book or any project: you have no control over how it will be understood or received. Creativity involves the most profound act of surrender we can engage in, allowing something to pass through us. It's such a paradoxical experience, because we have to be fully involved and out of the way at the same time: prolonged engagement and surrender. We don't own the results of our creative acts. We don't own our imagination or what our imagination gives birth to.

Just watch Stephen Curry take a three-point shot. Some call that being in the zone. It doesn't happen only in athletics, but can appear in any part of our life: making love, making music, making stories. Being in the zone happens when we totally forget ourselves and yet remain totally conscious of the moment. That is creativity. That is self-transcendence. The theological word for this is *resurrection*. Out of death life comes, out of nothingness newness is born.

Creativity is an instrument of healing in our lives and for the planet. Perhaps the most healing gesture we can make is to imagine that we belong. Belonging heals the deep wound of homelessness, the original alienation upon which is predicated the conviction that we are destined for a lifetime of therapy, a lifetime of pursuing many modalities of healing. At some profound level, we are convinced that we are unhealable, eternally without a home. A friend told me that one day she awoke convinced that the capacity to imagine is at the heart of healing. I believe she is right. Creativity makes healing possible because it challenges us to visualize what our life could be like if we no longer had the physical, emotional, and spiritual limitations that keep us diseased.

I recall again the pear tree we had in our backyard in my hometown in Canada. I learned two things from that tree: if you pick a pear too early, it isn't any good, and if you leave it on the tree too long, it gets soft and rots. That was a lesson about creativity. There's a moment, a timing, in the creative process. Ideas need to ripen in us before they can be born. The idea of wellness needs to ripen in us before we can be healed. Creativity heals the hole in our troubled hearts; it is central to our human vocation.

The scriptures say we need to become children again. We do that by retrieving our imagination. It is a mystical experience. It is an experience that is nourished by support and freedom and that results in healing for ourselves and our planet.

The Call

There comes a time in life when a mysterious call echoes in your heart and calls you forward. You are called to shake off all inertia and respond to the mysterious voice echoing in the recesses of your awakening soul.

This voice calls out to you, "Now is the time to begin again. With a resurgence of energy and hope, embrace the only life that is yours to live."

This call, perhaps previously unrecognized, awakens a new awareness. Listen deeply to it at this uncertain time. Forge a new beginning that is aligned with the trajectory of your life purpose, which is woven into your ageless soul.

In this place of the great unfolding mystery, rest and imagine, and be prepared to begin again. Sensitive to the signs of this defining moment, plunge into the turbulent waters of your life. With your mind and heart immersed, venture forth into the fetal waters of your wondrous and unfinished life.

Now is the time for a great transition, a time to retrieve precious memories while anticipating your return to the land of your soul. Once again, take on a beginner's mind. Celebrate all that is new, promising, and free.

Listen, my friend, to the promptings of your heart. It is

never too late to embrace what is possible for you to do. Embark on the untrodden path. You belong here. You always belonged here, in this place you call home.

Candles in the Night

Today the world appears
silent and uninviting
to so many dislocated souls.

They feel lost in a world
that promises nothing
but the illusion of power,
money and public acclaim.

Today I ask,
is it not true
that God is present
in secular experience?

Today I ask,
is it not true
that the prophets of yesterday
live on among us?

I think of
Dr. Martin Luther King, Jr.,
Robert Kennedy,
Thomas Merton,
Oscar Romero
and so many more.

Their vision and courage
captivate our lives,
energize our souls.

Their spirits and wisdom
are candles in the night
to dispel the darkness
for each lost soul.

A Vision for Tomorrow

As our traditions have retreated from relevance, spirituality has erupted in the minds and hearts of people. As faith in institutions has decreased, spirituality has increased. We have a great opportunity now. We have the opportunity to give birth to a new culture, to create not just with a paintbrush but on the canvas of relationships. We can create a society in which women's voices are honored, indigenous peoples are revered, traditions are revitalized, and science becomes mysticism rather than materialism. We need a new vision that will evoke positive energy, that will celebrate mystery, that will respond to the incredible hunger we have for meaning in our lives. Thus, consciousness and conscience become compatible. In a re-sacralized world, silence and listening will be reverenced. The prophetic voice will become our own, and we will have the creativity and the courage to express it.

At this critical point in human history, it is time to realize that ambiguity is probably the clearest approach we can take to describe who we are in this time of accelerated change. M.C. Richards brought this into focus for me. When asked to talk about herself, this brilliant woman, known for her book on creativity entitled *Centering*, explained that ambiguity is the best strategy to use to describe oneself. It is a way to avoid labels or stereotypes. If you label yourself by saying, "I am a doctor or a lawyer or a priest," you immediately become the cultural icon for that profession, with all its limits and expectations. If, however, you announce yourself with a level of ambiguity, your true self will emerge, and your creative potential will be more fully realized. On a societal level, in these in-between times, fundamentalism results from the positing of absolutes where they do not exist. As mentioned by Diarmuid O'Murchu, this is instead a time to live with messiness and to accept that from the chaos will emerge new forms that will give focus to our lives.

It is a time to ponder what the divine wants us to create in this moment of history. Thomas Berry calls this a moment of grace, a moment where transformation is possible, where disruption provides opportunity rather than reasons for despair. It is a time to ingest the universe story, by reading, by reflection, by ritual, and by a new kind of literacy that sees in the natural world the face of the divine. It is a time to realize that we need to let go of the worldview upon which much of our society has been based. Out of this shattering of the dominant worldview the possibility for new life will emerge.

We need to look at the relationship between intimacy and contemplation. In popular culture, as well as in our personal lives, there is probably a lack of one of these. We need both intimacy, so that our soul doesn't dry up, and enough silence and contemplative time in which to grow our soul. Edward Schillebeeckx, OP, describes this dynamic when he writes, "Without prayer or mysticism, politics soon becomes cruel and barbaric; without political love, prayer or mysticism becomes sentimental or uncommitted interiority." If we can balance the two, I think that we have the key to a lifestyle that fosters both spiritual development and a peaceful world.

A new mystical and engaged spirituality will reenergize our traditions and make them more relevant. We need cultural as well as personal therapy. We need to deconstruct society, to return to our point of origin. Then we need to reconstruct our society with the ethical principles that the universe teaches us: to respect difference, honor interiority and inwardness, and promote relationship and community. That is the task of what I call *geo-justice*. Taking the dynamics of evolution, putting them into cultural form, and practicing them provides us with a template for justice. The universe teaches us about ethics. If we truly made use of those principles, perhaps we wouldn't need the Ten Commandments. Only then would our vision of tomorrow become one of harmony, balance, and peace.

Overflowing

Practice recognition.
Prepare a listening heart.
Become an apostle of the ear,
a prophetic voice.

Tell truth to power,
wisdom to the world.
Listen to the mystic.
Unless you let go,
you cannot renter.

Embrace the dark night.
Sink into nothingness.
Tell your story.
Embrace the wonder of creation.

Make us one again.
Become an evolving presence
in a stuck and static world.
Become a source of life
for all that is vibrant and new.

Friends of god and prophets,
source of beauty and surprise,
make a joyful noise,
celebrate the creation of this world.

Contemplation and Soul: Action/ Reflection

How is your heart opened and your soul stirred as you contemplate the awe and wonder of the universe and the galaxies of your soul?

In what ways has the experience of intimacy and solitude enhanced your capacity to give full and conscious attention to your experience of ultimate mystery?

How through moments of contemplation, trusting your body, being willing to engage with others, and embracing the present moment have you been able to overcome the fear that blocks your capacity to experience the inmost recesses of your soul and to find your place in community?

What actions will energize and enhance your capacity to respond to the longing for intimacy and contemplation that resides in the universe and in your own soul?

Rediscovering Soul

To truly discover who we really are we must engage in a search:

- For a sacrament of engagement through which our work for equality and justice becomes an act of love

- For the subtle presence of the divine, who—as we discover with our new awareness—is already there

- For a new sensitivity to the poor and disadvantaged, whose vulnerability somehow reveals a transparency that allows the divine presence to shine through

- To penetrate and transform the negative energy and bitterness that are so often present in the struggle for integral ecology

- To extend our internal sensitivity beyond self to embrace the other and the Earth

- To savor silence and discover there increased clarity, focus, and self-esteem

- To discover the currents of inner wisdom that foster our attentiveness to dreams, imagination, and the unspoken language of God

- For increased energy in the struggle, an enhanced sense of community, and the time to explore a greater sense of purpose

- To heal the hunger in the emptiness and find recognition in relationship

- For our generational task, to discover soul in the great work as we listen attentively to the little ones of God and discover there a spirituality that will nurture engagement and a culture of hope

Grow Your Soul

Flags at half mast,
children dying,
the pop-pop of bullets
shatter the silence.
Guns terrorize our land.

When will the madness cease,
assassins put away their guns
and pick up a paint brush instead?

Set your spirit free.
Let it splash across your empty page,
colors of freedom and peace.

I hear the young say,
"Never again."
Listen to their voices.
Let violence cease.
Grow a soul of peace.

AT THE EDGE OF LIFE

A Canticle to Life

We awaken, as if for the first time,
to life as primary sacrament;
to a new life of ecology, community, and wisdom;
to a life of reciprocity, gratefulness, and awe;
to a life of cosmic common vision, creativity, and
    reverence;
to a life of natural beauty, mysticism,
and opportunity for the great work and integral presence;
to a life that is holistic,
that sees with new eyes the divine goodness everywhere;
to a life where education is a spiritual practice
that celebrates both intimacy and contemplation;
to a life where we witness and therefore become;
to a life whose culture is being brought to boil
in and through the cosmological imagination that bursts
    forth
from the heart of humanity
and the heart of the cosmos itself;
to a world of gratitude for good companions on the way
and the awakening hunger for life
that resides in the hearts of the young;
to a new world that we can call home,
a vision that will energize the next generation
so that we can become a people of gratitude and glory
for all that has been, is, and will be.

In this new life,
we will marry mind and the soul,
the cognitive and the moral.

Together we will give birth
to a re-enchanted cosmos;
to a new liberating spirituality,
to a new genesis;
to a new civilization;
to a new moment of grace;
to a new sense of destiny
founded on a sustainable future
where peace with Earth
makes possible peace on Earth
in a simultaneous embrace;
to a peace that is possible
through an enduring journey
of courage, joy, celebration, and ecstasy.

Wellspring of Life

To become vulnerable, to experience deeply, to risk rejection so we can grow will bring us more fully to the edge of our longing for life. It is here that our heart cries out. The poet Rilke writes, "Flare up like a flame and make big shadows I can move in." As our defenses melt, our hearts ignite more fully with passion, and all that is hidden can emerge. We reach out and open ourselves to relationship, to life. In our vulnerability, we embrace paradox, beauty, and terror, and dance courageously into the depths of self-discovery and life. With Rilke we say, "Nearby is the country they call life. You will know it by its seriousness. Give me your hand."

And so we journey with openness and trust into the uncharted future. With gratitude and praise, we celebrate each precious moment, each opportunity to quench our thirst for life. These eternal longings are the compass for the journey to the wellspring that, as Teilhard de Chardin puts it, we "dare to call our life." This interior compass guides us forward into the depths of our emotional truth. A compass, unlike a map that already has the destination marked out, continues to guide us through an ever-changing and unfolding journey.

Separation

"Angel of God, my Guardian dear,
to whom His love commits me here."
These are the opening words
of a prayer I learned as a child.

Today the media on radio, TV and print
is inundated with outcries of outrage and pain
announcing the separation being inflicted
on children and parents alike.
Echoes of fascism spill into today's news
and flow into every broken heart.

As today we witness "man's inhumanity to man"
through misplaced political force,
I join the chorus of outrage that overflows
from the conscience of the people.

I glance at the prayer card in my hand
and read the closing words:
"Ever this day be at my side,
to light and guard,
to rule and guide.
Amen."

Heal a Divided World

The great challenge for our lives is to live without separation or dualism. We seek to heal separateness, both in our lives and in the world. We could say our vocational purpose is to heal a divided world that challenges us to be makers of wholeness.

Together we make this prayer: "May we be one. May we be healed. Make us one again."

As agents of the oneness of mind and body, of the rational and the intuitive, we pursue interdisciplinary healing through the practices of contemplation and action. Our acts of healing separation will lessen the fragmentation of the world and unify the either-or experience.

With the integrative practices of our evolutionary faith, we open our hearts and minds and become integration people. We unite the past and the future so we can live harmoniously in an evolutionary world. We unite our stories and dreams and become healers of the either-or-ness of our society, which propagates divisions between the rich and the poor, female and male, abstraction and sacred work.

The mystics advise us to be patient with all the divisions in our world and to practice a spirituality that unleashes vitality and creativity. Such a spirituality affirms diversity and is noncompetitive. It allows us to lay aside our defenses and become one people.

We become agents of our own destiny and zealous contributors to peace and justice in this world.

We become people whose souls can lose themselves in life's wonderful enchantment.

Amen.

State of the World

Things as we know them
are falling apart.
We live today in the dark night
of our cultural soul.

The lack of good work
erodes the spirit
of a society driven
by corporate greed.

We must make drastic change,
create opportunities
for all people,
pick up the pieces of beauty.

Reimagining Our Future

How are we related to life, to Earth, to the divine? How do we discover where we are, to gain guidance for the future? How do we take up our roles to be leaders in the twenty-first century?

When our ancestors began their prophetic work with its particular challenges, the times were different and the great work of those moments were unique to the time.

Wars have been won and lost.

Land has been cultivated and cleared.

Transportation has gone from the horse and buggy to the jet.

Conflict among nations and peoples has shifted from spears to smart bombs, preemptive strikes, and collateral damage.

Our region has gone from a healthy environment to a time of genocide, fertilizers, and industrial agriculture.

Agriculture has moved from family gardens to agribusiness.

Technology has given us great gifts and also been instrumental in unimagined destruction.

The information age has changed the world.

Communication has moved from courier pigeon to e-mail.

Health care has changed from family doctors to state-funded delivery systems.

We have moved from a time when our ancestors awoke in the morning and knew where they were to a time of cultural Alzheimer's, where people lose their way on the planet

Education has gone from one-room schools to distance learning and international student exchange.

Clothing has shifted from traditional habits to street clothes.

Religion has moved from catechism to the cosmos.

As we reflect on the legacy of the past, we ask, "What are our challenges today?" As we review the accomplishments as well as the tragedies and missteps of the past, we realize there is much more to be accomplished.

Our great work is revealed by the challenge to respond

with courage and compassion to this unprecedented moment in human/Earth history. Our call to the great work is born out of the wisdom of the medieval mystic Meister Eckhart, who named ministry as "whatever needs to be done."

Our call is to become instruments of health and wholeness. It is an invitation to heal both the planet and ourselves. It is a call for pure water, clean air, healthy livestock, and a wholesome Earth.

Our call is to nurture and support the dignity of the child and the wisdom of the elder and to all of us who inhabit this sacred land. It is a call for wisdom and depth: a call to teach our children the wonders of creation, to invite each child to look to the stars and understand that they behold the bonfire of their ancestors.

Our call to perceive in the poor and forsaken a special presence of the divine.

Our call is to engagement, to an engaged spirituality. It is a call to retrieve and celebrate the wisdom of the entire community of life, a call to respond to the crises and challenges of our time, as we align our energy to the unfolding dynamics of the universe and become catalysts for justice in an uncaring world.

We are invited to hear and respond to the call of justice: to connect the stars to the street, to comprehend the connection between the crack in the ozone layer and the crack sold in the street.

Our call is an invitation to altruism and generosity. It is a time to transcend narrow self-interest and be enchanted by the generosity of the sun. It is a time for bigheartedness, when with magnanimity, our hearts open and our imagination soars. It is a time of interconnectedness and inter-being.

Our call is an invitation to experience freedom and volcanic eruptions of the soul as we set about letting all the captives free. It is an invitation to resurgence and regeneration, wherein our collective work makes possible emergence, beauty, and new life. It is an invitation to weave together a membrane of compassion that dispels despair and reignites the original fire, to illuminate the dark night of our cultural soul. It is an invitation to a deep resonance with all of life when, with all artists, we will share the profound experience of how it feels to be free. It is an invitation to celebrate and realize that hope is not a conviction that something will turn out well, but a deep certainty that something makes sense and is worth doing, regardless of how it turns out.

A Call Within the Call

When our calling comes, we might be asked to take our life into our own hands just when things seem least clear to us. Pain and loss often open the door to our true self. Something in us tells us we've been off course. When we become physically ill, we know there's something wrong. The same thing is true of our life's direction. If we're troubled in our hearts, then something is off course.

Often the very significant things that change our life seem insignificant at the moment they happen. But when we look back later, we recognize them as turning points. It could have been a phone call, a gesture, an insight, a trip—any moment when we took a new direction, when we knew what we had to do, and began.

The voice of vocation doesn't lead us to exactly where our heroes have been. We're not here to be another Gandhi or King or Teresa of Avila or Mother Teresa. Though we might be inspired by such people, inspiration is not authentic if it leads only to a rigid imitation. The challenge is not to repeat their lives but to learn how they brought them about, how they changed the culture to make their vision a possibility. That's the kind of imitation our ancestors are calling us to.

How can we be true to ourselves? Mary Oliver says you are here "determined to save the only life you could save." To me, that means being true to your inner wisdom, promptings, indicators, to the moments of synchronicity and those sacred impulses that guide you toward the future. Most of us have tapes inside us—the voices of our parents, of institutions, of authority figures—that have conditioned us to respond in ways that are less than authentic. What is authentic is often what we know for certain without being able to explain why. From that knowing, we stride deeper and deeper into the world. "To save the only life you could save" is to answer your calling. Ironically, it is through saving ourselves that we earn the capacity to save others.

Vocation in our world is usually associated with a job. We define ourselves by our functions, our professions. But we are not what we do for a living. One of the ways to ask ourselves what we're called to is to see what we are preoccupied with, what we are passionate about, what we are competent in. What are our gifts? What are we committed to? The call to a deeper life is not about the external lifestyle choices we have made. It's not about our religious life or whether we are married or single. It's about the call within the call, about what summons each of us to be our authentic self.

From Doorbells to Beauty

Doorbell rings.
It's a person from the street,
Hungry, disheveled, lost,
without answers or solutions.

I press a voucher into his hand,
point to a kitchen down the street,
say a soft goodbye, without much thought,
go inside and close the door.

Later I hear another knock,
a victor of the AA journey
invites my friendship and support
to make possible a place
of recovery and rest for the homeless.

As an offspring of the famine people,
I feel close in my heart
to every hungry and alienated soul
who inhabits this monastery of the lost.

I honor the lost souls
as their turbulent days unfold,
awash in oceans of urban pain,
among the vanquished of the street.

In this forlorn place,
I listen with my heart and say,
"I saw Christ today

in this world of violence and fear."

I feel the deep divides
that tear the tattered world apart.
Here, I once again tell the story
inscribed in the beauty
of the lily of the fields.

With my cousins of creation,
I pray songs of gratitude
for so much beauty,
for every unique gift,
for each communion with glory.

Empowered and embraced
by the triune God,
wonderous rivers of grace
awaken each beating heart
to songs of praise
for our great unfinished melody of life.

Revitalizing Art

I arrive today,
heart full of wonder,
hope overflowing,
enveloped in mystery.

I gaze into wonder
as everyone gathered here
sings salutations to Earth.

Songs of melody and thunder
echo in the chamber of each story,
become a bandshell of beauty,
sending ripples of memories,
now and until we part.

Remembrance

We remember
and make present
the little ones of God.
In our recollection,
we proclaim that poverty
is not their destiny.

The denial
of significance
is a condition of injustice,
a doorway to death,
a challenge to courageously
go against the grain.

Life is transformed.
We engage in creative action,
celebrate beauty,
experience hope,
and are healed in our longing
for unconditioned love.

Engagement and Action

We live today in a time where society is marked by indicators of withering and decay, a time when institutions oppose their original purposes, a time when the efforts of good people with the best of intentions often produce the opposite of their intended results.

Generous people are being called to create a context of support where their destinies are not defeated, to build a bridge into the future. It will be a bridge of transition and change: a bridge of new eras, new paradigms and a new world view. It will be a time to create clusters of generosity where people gather and reflect on approaches that fulfill their deeper purpose and build a vibrant Earth community.

Through conscientious action we create culture and build a bridge into the new era that awaits us. We become visually literate, see the world as it is, and are committed to recreate the world as we would like it to be. With Dr. Martin Luther King, Jr., we are convinced that "the arc of the universe is long and bends toward justice." Our action becomes a celebration of the interdependence of all things, freedom for all sentient beings, and the primary revelation that is present everywhere in creation. Through conscious engagement, we become infused with a renewed ability to act. Through reciprocity and trust, we imagine and create a world where beauty can shine forth.

It is a time to evoke and articulate a vision of a better to-morrow, a time to compose and live out beatitudes for the new creation in order to heal and energize the wounds of soul, society, and Earth.

Empowerment

May I be empowered
to heal what is broken,
to celebrate oneness
in every faith and form.

May I be a unifying force
amidst all who pray
and hope for love
here in a shattered world.

May I always
anticipate each new tomorrow,
may my words become actions
that heal and unite.

Fresh and Ancient Stories

May the wisdom of the ages
call out from the depths
of every grateful heart.

As radical engagement
flows forth like a refreshing fountain,
we celebrate each breakthrough,
bringing newness to the world.

May we rejoice at each new chance
to give our life away,
as fresh and ancient stories
call us home again.

Expectations

Long histories
seem short-sighted.
Strive for a collective purpose
to heal the separateness of life.

With a passion for healing,
a flare for life,
creativity challenges and
new possibilities occur.

Take up the challenge.
Resolve conflicts.
Step outside the expected.
Pursue a common search.

Welcome the invitation
to a deep and intuitive life.
Unlock you imagination.
Transform the conformity of life.

Embrace each opportunity.
Recreate what's past.
Become a world of change.
Dare to create the impossible.

Invite others to do the same.

Our Tangled World

We live today
in a culture of unrest.
In politics and the evening news,
conflict, insult and turbulence unfold.

Almost every day,
week by week,
month by month,
year by year.

We feel the conflict in our hearts,
pain in the people,
as we sink more deeply
into each diminishing moment.

Now is the time
to live again,
to challenge the pulse
of each new day.

Rise above the problems
and heal the dismay.
Each day is an opportunity
to become entirely new.

Untangle the knots
of this tortured world.
Live with hope.
Enact a sacred time.

Gestures of the Heart

The group of my students and I exited the BART (Bay Area Rapid Transit) station and hurried to St. Boniface Church in San Francisco's Tenderloin district to begin our day with the city's homeless. We discovered there the home of roughly 28,000 people living in a fourteen-square block area, a district bordered by the power structures of this internationally recognized city nestled on the San Francisco Bay: the Civic Center (political), Nob Hill (social), and Union Square (commercial).

As Mary Ann Finch of the Care Through Touch Institute welcomed us to our urban plunge, we became palpably aware of the love that is extended to and expressed daily by these "little ones of God," these people of the Tenderloin who spend their days sleeping in the park, waiting for a meal, and bouncing around the health-care system in an often-futile attempt to receive medical attention. These homeless ones are consistently sheltered by the open hearts of those who each day befriend and dissolve the terror of exile and alienation that festers in the cell blocks of the street.

As we stood in line that day and joined the multitude who are served meals daily by St. Anthony's Foundation, stories of pain, isolation, and yet great dignity were told. The narratives of broken lives and shattered dreams poured forth, prompted not only by physical hunger but also by a deeper longing for meaning, purpose, pride, and life. Yet amidst the many sacred stories we heard that day, we felt with ever-greater cadence pulsations of compassion from those whom society seems too willing to discard.

On our day in the Tenderloin, we went back to school. In our inner-city classroom, we discovered as if for the first time that joy lives in the streets where we were introduced to homeless persons. They became our teachers, our mentors, and our guides. As they introduced us to the agencies and people who serve the Tenderloin, we were gifted with more stories: stories of remarkable courage, stories of beauty and brokenness, gestures of the heart that heal pain and build bridges of friendship.

To complete the day, we gathered in a circle at the Care Through Touch Institute. Our teachers from the Tenderloin, with great gratitude and moving pride, shared their experiences of the day. This sacred event transcended previous moments of broken marriages, rejection by families, endless nights on park benches, untreated illness, and multiple addictions. At that moment, we were enveloped in a membrane of hope and love. In this circle of compassion, our teachers taught us again to laugh, to listen, and to cry. They taught us to transcend the symbols of power that surround the Tenderloin and permeate our lives. They reminded us that "God is present in the poor." We discovered from our teachers that divinity lives in the Tenderloin and other places of poverty, and that its address can be found in gestures of the heart.

As my students and I returned to the street and entered the nearest BART station, the lyrics of our "song of the day" echoed in our hearts: "I will never leave you. I will always love you. I will always keep you in my heart."

Jim Conlon

Beatitudes for the New Creation

Blessed are the contemplatives:
they shall experience the longing of the soul.

Blessed are the liberators:
they shall experience the longing of life.

Blessed are the earthlings:
they shall experience the longing of creation.

Blessed are those who long for God:
they shall experience
the interdependence of contemplation,
the freedom of liberation,
the beauty of the new creation.

Young People Rise Up

I join the people of Parkland, Florida, as they mourn the loss of precious lives taken from their families and friends by the misguided, violent rage of a young man.

I share the tragic moment of a heartbroken mother who is asked to pick out a dress for her daughter's funeral. Now she will never look forward to the day when she and her daughter pick out a wedding dress.

The students cry in one voice, "Enough!" Enough killing. Enough pain. Enough sorrow and loss. As they mobilize to march on Washington, their voices are heard around America.

"Never again," I hear them say. How long must we weep over the stolen lives of our people because of the cultural pathology of gun violence in this country?

This plea for peace follows me into my sleep. In a dream, I meet someone who was important in my life, but from whom I became estranged. However, in the dream, we reconcile. Forgiveness is granted, and gifts are given and received. It is truly a peacemaker's dream.

The next morning, I feel moved all the more strongly to join with the hearts and minds of the youth of America, to listen to their courageous voices calling us to be a people of peace.

This Peace Will Say Yes

We join with all who are willing
to speak truth to power,
that together we may begin to realize
a growing movement for peace.

This peace will be more than a truce.
This peace will recognize
that the price of every gun
is a theft from the poor.

This peace will give us the courage
to stand up for freedom,
to take back our country.
This peace will heal all separation
and celebrate the sheer joy of living.

This peace will say yes
to reverence, dialogue, sensitivity.
This peace will say yes
to economic and educational security
and affordable housing security.

This peace will say no
to violence, competition, war.
This peace will say no
to the terrorism of poverty, ignorance,
homelessness, racism, imperialism,
and ecological devastation.

This peace will say yes
to mercy, kindness, forgiveness, cooperation,
and a convergence of the heart.
This peace will say yes
to a culture rooted
in a new religious sensitivity.

Today in America

Politics has been called the art of the possible. Some say the first act of politics is compromise. Others say you campaign with poetry and govern with prose. Today in America, I ponder the place of poetry in our discourse and I mourn its absence in the news of the day.

As I glance at the television screen and gaze into the well of the Senate, I see men and (a few) women who have been entrusted with the fate of our nation seemingly unable to do what I believe Thomas Merton meant when he said, "True poems seem to live by a life entirely their own." What would it take, I wonder, for politicians to "live by a life entirely their own"?

I feel the need to search for the wisdom available in lyrical language and am encouraged by the words of Derek Walcott, who wrote many years ago, "The fate of poetry is to fall in love with the world in spite of history." Today, we might say "in love with the Earth," as well.

During this time of danger and anxiety, perhaps poetry can provide a new way of seeing—as the art form of the mystic and the clarion call of the prophet, and as the voice of the women and men who take to the streets, in the hope that tomorrow may be a time when life, liberty, and the pursuit of happiness flourish on Earth.

Stand Up

Today I stand up
for the sacramentality of existence.

I give great thanks
and say how proud I am
to claim my inheritance.
I send hopeful salutations
to all who pray for courage,
solidarity and love.

Immersed in the pain that ravages
people, water and land,
may we become more aware
that the call for justice
is constitutive of the gospel,
and care for our common home
is integral to a well-lived life.

Books!

I have an affinity for books. The books in my collection are my friends. They contain the words and wisdom of people I admire. They contain memories and stories, and doorways into unexpected moments.

In today's digital age, smartphones and laptops and the Internet provide an easy means of communication. But not everyone is using them to read books. Books remain a valued source of wisdom. I glance at the bookshelves in my room and recall the titles of published works I value. In each, a thoughtful writer has commented on the significance of global events and offered insights into the causes and consequences of life-changing times.

Books are my good companions. They keep me company, along with Shelley the dog, here at the Pine Cottage in the Hermitage, among the trees in South Carolina, that I now dare to call home.

Liberation and Life: Action/Reflection

What encounters with people, and nature, have deepened your desire to ponder the meaning of freedom and existence?

What holds you back from being fully present and engaging in a life of freedom and fulfillment for every species?

How have these moments of intimacy nurtured your efforts to be an instrument of liberation for people and the planet?

In what way has creativity deepened your capacity in the art of life?

Rediscovering Life

To plumb the mysterious depths of life we must:

- Plunge into the deepest recesses of the human heart and the heart of the universe

- Play, pray, act, reflect, write, create, relate, dialogue, remain silent, and become newly aware of and connected to the person we can become, and more fully realize the deeper purpose of our existence and calling

- Become fully immersed in and critically aware of our toxic culture, yet not obsessed by it, so that we can learn to create clarity in our imagination and focus in our heart as we strive to become delivered to our self and transform toxicity into justice

- Surrender to the wild energy of the cosmos, whose power and potential take us to a new level of uncertainty and surprise, where the universe, activated by the divine creative energy, can do its work and we can do ours

- Relax, don't force the river, while creating the capacity to become fully focused and engaged, yet detached from the outcome

Pledge Allegiance

I pledge allegiance
to preserve and protect
our common home,
to unite mind and heart,
to celebrate integral wisdom,
to bring hope and anticipation
to tomorrow
as if it were today.

I pledge allegiance
to this enduring quest
for a healed and wholesome world.
May we be one
with all that is unsolved
in our lives,
as ambivalence fades
into wonder
on each mysterious day.

Together We Can Forge

Together we can forge
a culture of confidence and depth,
a culture of compassion and admiration,
a culture of beauty and identity for each participant,
a culture of concern and reciprocity,
a culture of creativity and engagement,
a culture of gratitude and collaboration,
a culture of struggle and fulfillment,
a culture of challenge and change,
a culture of action and reflection,
a culture of story and deep listening,
a culture of justice and reverence for the voiceless,
a culture of flexibility and focus,
a culture of transcendence and transformation,
a culture of tenderness and strength,
a culture of intimacy and contemplation,
a culture of amazement and mutuality,
a culture of listening and recognition,
a culture of mysticism and engagement.

t

AT THE EDGE OF EARTH

A Canticle to Earth

An integral and engaged spirituality
takes us to the edge of our longings for Earth.

This Earth spirituality is responsive
to interior and external challenges.

This Earth spirituality has the capacity
to read the signs of the times on our poisoned planet.

This Earth spirituality is not unduly obsessive
so our clarity does not become clouded
or our hope in danger of despair.

This Earth spirituality has the practice
of avoiding an activism whose overemphasis
dislocates us from our center
and diminishes our engagement.

This Earth spirituality provides access to fresh energy
by engaging in unmediated mysticism
through which we experience oneness
with self, life, creation, and the divine.

Sacred Soil

The earth is alive.
It bursts forth today,
a metaphor for all that lives.

The earth bursts forth
in sunshine and in rain,
once again, a garden of new life.

This sacred soil,
the source of wisdom,
the source of all that lives.

Each morsel of your flesh,
alive with a liberating call,
shouting hope to the world.

On High and Earth Below

Songs of grateful salutations
float across the sky,
settle in the recesses of my soul.
Grateful one,
source of beauty, love and life
you are that place
from which all good flows.

Send salutations
to the mountains
and the meadows below.
Envision a sacred place of rest.
In slumber and in solitude,
there is a new state of mind:
all is holy, replete with fresh awareness.

Each quiver in my soul
overflows into wonder and surprise.
Today I pray,
may each trembling and uncertain tomorrow,
all that pulsates,
and all that longs to live
become awash in peace.

Imagine

Imagine a world in which we cross over into a thundering new awareness, a time when we emerge into the flood of a vast new understanding.

Imagine yourself gathering among a cluster of colleagues who declare to our endangered planet, "We are your first responders. We are here as planetary people to bring healing, to tell our story at this terminal phase of human/ Earth history."

Now is the time to look back and imagine how things came to be as they are, to see how they are now, and to move from diagnosis to becoming a healing people dedicated to respond to the cry of the Earth.

I invite you to imagine a wonderous future in which every sacred impulse will call us forth, to imagine a new world order where everything is holy, where every culture, language, color, rock, meadow, and tree can become a new paragraph in the great story.

When we ingest this joyful wisdom bubbling up from the recesses of our imagination, a fresh new ocean of grace will pour forth to accomplish whatever needs to be done. Beauty will call us forward as we are seized by the vision of a future not yet imagined.

The Willow

This expansive place
welcomes pilgrims
who dare to search for home,
for a gentle, peaceful rest.

This weeping willow
offers hope to those
who long to put down roots,
who choose to save the Earth.

Meadow Time

Earth is a sacrament,
a divine presence
that permeates your soul,
envelops your awareness.

Perhaps a memory
an engaging recollection,
has bathed you
in a living, energizing presence.

Sink deeply
into a sacred recollection
of when you felt touched
by the wonder of it all.

Promise

See light in the window
as dawn breaks through again,
the stars recede in vast opaqueness,
while the moon reclines and rests.

Another day begins,
and the sacrament appears:
a turtle on the beach,
a deer on the lawn.

A bird cries in her nest,
eager for breakfast
from her mother's beak,
a promise of delight.

Great Tree of Life

The tree of life
is shelter in the storm,
standing elegant
in sunshine and in rain.

Rooted in the great story,
you rise up and
extend your branches,
heal our planet's wounds,
bathe us in beauty all around.

You are the tree of life.
Dance in the fields.
Celebrate the presence
of every flower and bird
in the meadow of new life.

Like each plant,
spider and bird,
join the chorus.
Proclaim with joy
the mystery we call our life.

Bioregions: A Compass for the Journey

I've found it helpful to use the concept of bioregion to draw out the implications of our relationship with life and with all creation. A bioregion is a self-contained dimension of the Earth, bounded by waterways, trees, and hill lines and defined by the Earth itself. For example, I was born in the Great Lakes bioregion on the St. Clair River, which unites Lake Huron and Lake St. Clair.

A context for life. A bioregion is a complex structure made up of differentiated but mutually supportive life systems that are self-sustaining. Some characteristics of a bioregion are especially relevant to our understanding of how we should relate to one another and to our environment.

A context for self-propagation. The first such characteristic is self-propagation. If a bioregion is going to be healthy, every species has to have space to sustain life, to build its house, so to speak. The same thing applies for the human community: we need enough space to be surrounded, room for both intimacy and contemplation. Living with others doesn't mean that you don't need and want privacy. Living alone doesn't mean that you don't need and want community. To receive what we need and long for, we must understand the needs and wants of the creatures with whom we share the space, and negotiate so that nothing and no one is left out.

A context for reciprocity. A bioregion is also self-nourishing. One of the great examples of the self-nourishing universe is the relationship between a mammal and a tree. A mammal exhales carbon dioxide and inhales oxygen, while a tree takes in carbon dioxide and gives off oxygen. That's why we get into such a mess when we cut down the rainforest: our very ability to breathe is compromised. In the human community, we also need a balance between extroverts and introverts; we need both people who can go off on their own for the day and others who need company. We need to respect our differences but also realize that a certain amount of reciprocity is required. "I'll cultivate the potatoes because if they mature, I'll have food for the winter." The universe operates like that. In this way, entropy, the loss of energy within the system, is minimized.

A context for guidance. The third characteristic of a bioregion is that it is self-educating. A few decades ago, Catholics interested in growing spiritually had spiritual directors. In the old days, a spiritual director sometimes was thought to be the voice of God telling you what to do. I think the universe itself can be our best spiritual director when we are able to engage in its rhythms in ways that evoke and create responses in us. Our pets can even provide spiritual guidance. If you have a cat, the cat knows exactly what's going on with you. Cats come up to you if you're sad and leave you alone if you're angry. Pets are like that. So is the whole universe. We can learn so much from living interdependently with all of life and learning from the bioregions that surround us. To sit under a catalpa tree and write poetry could be a wonderful exercise in spiritual guidance.

A context for healing. This leads us into another dimension of bioregions: they are self-healing. The medical profession is predisposed to operate and remove a dysfunctional part rather than return it to a harmonious relationship with the whole. If you look at how your body works, how the Earth works, however, they have the capacity for self-healing. If you cut your finger, it will most likely heal itself. This is equally true of the soul and psyche. What's needed is to stimulate the psyche so that healing can take place. We need to be sensitive to each other so that healing can be maximized for everyone. We need to both respect each person's journey and challenge each other in a loving way. We need to respect and support this same self-healing in the plants, animals, minerals, and bacteria with whom we share this planet, so that a truly healthy ecosystem can emerge as a home for all of us.

When we integrate these characteristics of bioregions into our lives—by self-propagating, self-nourishing, self-educating, self-healing and self-emerging—we respond to a deep longing to experience this planet as our home.

Earth and Creation

Beyond the longing of soul and life,
resides a deeper hunger within
each member of the Earth community;
a longing for intimacy, relationship,
and enchantment with Earth.
Each species,
with its particular gifts and desire to interact,
invites admiration.
At the very heart of each being resides
the essence of its existence and the capacity to relate.
The very Earth desires to commune
with its individuated self,
be it animal, vegetable or mineral.
The longing of Earth is engaged in
through the revelatory moments
that happen when we experience Earth
through our senses.
In sight, sound, touch and smell,
we listen to the language and longings
of creation.

Fresh Oil Again

Air is fresh,
sky so blue,
heaven wonderous,
Earth sacred too.

Today beyond age,
occasion and context,
hold out conviction that
tomorrow is different;
as Gregory Baum says,
"the oil has not run dry."

Change is possible.
Beauty evolves.
Society and soul
are no longer separate.

Trust remains important
for prolonged engagement,
that each new tomorrow
may flourish and fade,
only to rise again
as each new day
becomes wonderous,
amazing and true.

A Village of Hope

Earthaven Ecovillage is nestled in the mountains of North Carolina, just outside the city of Asheville. Within this unassuming yet daring experiment, I saw glimpses of the world that our deepest longing calls us to build. From the time I first heard of it, I felt called to visit this experiment of living within the dynamics of the Earth.

At Earthaven, men, women, and children are discovering new ways to build homes, to access power, and to gain a livelihood. They are totally off the commercial electric grid. Their energy is solar, they grow their own food, they build their own homes. This shared activity affords them a space for both privacy and relationship, contemplation and intimacy. Earthaven is an intergenerational community whose goal is to live in a mutually enhancing manner with the land. Through courage, imagination, and commitment, they dedicate their labor to sustainability.

One Sunday evening, I joined them in their community center, a thirteen-sided building whose architecture reflects the Mayan solar calendar. There, I met people who had followed their dreams to participate in this prototype for the future of our race. They have made a radical break with the consumerism of the dominant American culture and live a life of simplicity in order to build a better world for their children. Their lifestyle does not come at the price of pollution or depletion of the Earth's finite resources.

Following the introductions, we began our dialogue by relating the story of the universe and its transformations—from the initial fireball to the galactic, Earth, life, and human periods—in order to create a context in which to place the personal narratives of Earthaven and its creators. The responses were powerful, spontaneous, and moving. One of the early members told of the original formulation of the dream, of the shattering of previous attempts, and how the group had finally secured the property on which Earthaven is built. Subsequently, others chimed in about how they came to join this adventure and what brought them to this sacred place, now a beacon of hope.

As we listened to the stories of how people felt called to Earthaven, it seemed to me that they were cultural canaries driven from the toxicity of the outside world to form a sustainable community. One man told of riding his bicycle across the country to take a course in permaculture, only to remain and raise a family. Some spoke of searching for a way of life apart from the consumption-mad world. Others recounted their disenchantment with corporate America, and their deep desire to live intentionally. Some of the older people announced that having raised their families, they were free to live in the manner they had always wished. As the stories continued, they were punctuated by laughter and moments of clarity. With arduous effort and great hope, people were fashioning an eco-village, a new way of living. They were literally beginning again. With a sensitivity to the Earth, a new vision of lifestyle and livelihood was emerging.

We had begun the evening by coming together in a circle singing the chant "If we're here for anything at all, it's to take care of the Earth!" As we dispersed at the end of the evening, the chant reverberated in my ears and I felt very connected to this noble experiment that challenges us to dream new dreams, imagine new lives.

Jim Conlon

Where Spirits Dwell

Gospel of beauty,
hymns of my heart,
listen to the vast cloud sing
from the billowing sky above.

Become my compass,
ignite my soul,
here on God's green Earth,
where all spirits dwell.

Tall Trees

Trees so tall,
forest so deep,
the broken Earth
is why I weep.

On this wild day,
I listen to spirit speak,
in these silent woods.

Once more, I ask spirit
to whisper to us,
as sacred seekers,
to tell us what's next
in this dark time,
to show us the way.

Running Water

Do you remember a time when you were thirsty, and what it felt like to take that first sip of cool, fresh water? Perhaps it was after a vigorous sporting event. Someone offered you a glass of water, and you rejoiced as the cool liquid trickled down your throat and quenched your thirst.

The gift of water may quench our physical thirst, but thirst comes to us in so many ways. We experience thirst as a deeper longing. Just as we long for food to nourish our body, for example, we long for friendship when we are lonely. We long to end pain and suffering. We long for meaning and purpose in our lives.

In the midst of our longing lies a consistent and enduring theme. This theme is notably found in the words of Brother David Steindl-Rast, who describes our seemingly unquenchable thirst as a search for "the More" and points out that "we will always want to have something else or something more."

As I set aside my paper and pen and turn on the radio to listen to the news of the day, I almost unknowingly and without intention ingest the anxiety of our polarized world: the war in Syria; conflicts across the Middle East; gun violence in school classrooms; and the precarious state of the many undocumented, whose lives are soaked in uncertainty.

In the next moment, an unbidden awareness floods the landscape of my soul. I rejoice in the realization that today, as planetary people who live in the midst of turmoil, we can be reconciled and healed as we move forward to quench our thirst for "the More" as we take the balm of love that is like running water to the soul and mend what is broken, bring peace, overcome injustice, and renew the face of the Earth.

Listen to the River

Listen to the river
echo in my heart.

On this St. Clair day,
I voyage upstream,
where elements of life abound.
Buoyant, refreshing moments
activate dangerous memories,
manifest in rainbows to the world.

From the channel bank,
my heart leaps
in sacred salutations
of wordless wisdom,
announcing news
of our planetary soul.

To the Sea

The ocean, so engulfing,
healing and deep,
is a poultice for poison,
a source of great strength,
a context for beauty,
as it refreshes all our lives.

Imagining Newness

Energy flows like molten lava,
as the imagination erupts,
and from this place
of birth and possibility,
a new creation is born.
The heart of the universe unfolds
as we begin to pulsate
with all that is possible.
Our world continues to unfold
and much that is new shows up.
Let there be light in the darkness,
peace in war,
sunshine at dawn,
wonder in day
and reverence at dusk,
as we seek an enduring peace.

Our Chapter in the Story

As we gaze upon the beauty resulting from the volcanic eruptions and the enchanting landscape of bushlands and beaches, of valleys and mountaintops, we ponder again the great history of the universe and reflect on our common origin. From this place, we know deeply that we are all shaped and formed in that same primordial furnace, and we feel energized again to endure the bitter and burdensome moments of life, the Gethsemane moments as we engage in the Paschal mystery story of our time—the life, death, and rebirth of our people and our planet here in the beauty of God's creation.

Our invitation at this time is to realize again that our work is a significant chapter in the great cosmic story, a story told in each of our lives and projects and heard daily through the stars and in the streets. It is an invitation to awaken again to the realization that where we stand determines what we see, and that our position on this planet is to stand with the children and the poor of every species on this sacred Earth. We are here to celebrate a new invitation, to create membranes of meaning, and embrace a new cosmic vision that will include imagination and wisdom, courage and engagement, intimacy and contemplation, trust and equanimity within the turbulence of new life.

We honor our ancestors, express gratitude for this present moment, and look toward the future with anticipation and hope.

It is a future inscribed in each of our hearts and punctuated by our participation in the great work, our participation in a mission.

It is a future incarnated in our commitment to partnership, participation, and protection.

It is a future that will be enhanced by a shared vision that nurtures dignity, identity, and respect.

It is a future that will be energized by the awe and wonder of an unfolding universe.

It is a future that honors and celebrates tenderness and strength, and is captured by the vision of a flower bursting through the concrete to bring beauty to a place neglected and oppressed.

We hold forth a vision that will be embraced in this new moment of justice, when we will create the conditions among us for beauty to blossom forth. It is a new moment when each person and each project will compose a sonnet of justice, a song of compassion, for Earth and every species. Each will become an instrument in the orchestra to intone the music of creation and compose a new chapter in the great story that calls us together.

The Promise

Energy rises,
converges in the sky.

Collaboration happens,
culture becomes cosmic.

Spontaneity bursts forth,
soul awakens.

An energetic ocean
pours forth onto humanity and Earth.

Intimacy and contemplation abound
in the longing for mystery and communion.

A search for parallel approaches
reveals the promise of a better world.

Jim Conlon

Sacred Beauty

Is it not possible
to see each person
as a friend?

See each one
without problems,
challenges and wounds.

Rather, see each one
with vision,
foresight and love.

Is it not possible
to become a friend,
to look past failure and pain?

See in each one
a secret beauty,
without worry,
anxiety or shame.
In each one,
discover sacred beauty,
wonder and awe.

Creation and Earth: Action/Reflection

What experiences of the other-than-human world have shaped your sense of the sacred and influenced the trajectory of your life?

How have the rhythms of each day and of the seasons—with the anticipation of spring, the abundance of summer, the vulnerable beauty of autumn, and the waiting of winter—animated your soul?

How has your relationship with the natural world awakened in you a desire to care for the Earth?

In what ways do you feel called to respond to the devastation of the Earth and resacralize creation?

How do you feel moved to respond with courage and respect to the promise and possibility present in each expression of creation?

Rediscovering Earth

Become planetary citizens of harmony, balance, and peace, we must become:

- People whose imaginations perceive a world of geo-justice and who hope for a better world for the children of every species

- People who perceive spirituality as a studio for personal, cultural, and ecological transformation

- People who are aligned with a more mutually enhancing future

- People who are deeply connected to the trajectory of our own story

- People who are find expression in a culture of compassion

- People who locate ourselves within the great drama of the universe and participate in creating a culture of hope embedded in the dynamics of the cosmos and its unfolding into life

- People with a deepened understanding of Earth as a living organism

- People who will discover a context in which life can be lived in a more meaningful way

- People with a deepened sense of place, and an increased insight into the wisdom traditions

- People who will create and redesign our work to advance ecological justice, planetary peace, and personal and social liberation

Jim Conlon

Venture Forth

Take up the challenge,
dear friends of holy mystery.
Engage in the struggle,
find fulfillment,
dynamically integrate
the original fire.
May it consume
all that is static.

Savor this sacred moment,
gaze into the live oak forest.
Listen to the rustle of the trees,
breathe a precious prayer
of gentle peace.

Call out to your cousins of creation,
call them by their true names:
Sister Sun, Brother Moon.
Celebrate the generosity of Earth.
Sing songs of gratitude and praise.
Welcome each tender voice.

Heal the unrest in society and soul.
Venture forth, dear friends,
may we sacred seekers,
empowered by the amazing goodness
of the great spirit,
take one more tender step,
enthusiastically encouraged
by each good companion.

At this new moment of grace,
sing songs.
May your new life
flow out with
each evolutionary heart,
bringing beauty
and belonging to the world.

Jim Conlon

AT THE EDGE OF THE DIVINE

A Canticle to the Divine

God of the cosmos,
source of soul, life, and Earth,
we come to you today,
wondering at the edge
of all for whom we pray.

Invigorate our spirit,
breathe enthusiasm
into all who dare to live,
celebrate sacredness
among us here today.

May the birth of wonder
at each Gethsemane moment
rise up and surprise us
on this wonderous day.

Now is the time, dear friends,
to let your soul speak,
come back to life,
become planetary people.

Find the source of uniqueness,
diversity, and life.
All the world is one!
All the world is one!

Quest for the Living God

Today I ask, "What gives meaning and purpose to your life?"

When I reflect on this question, I surrender my tendency to believe that I can know God the way I can solve a problem in mathematics. I acknowledge that God is a mystery I can only grasp intuitively and ponder in my imagination—an oceanic experience beyond conscious thought that resides in deep interiority.

Yes, each of us and all that exists is enveloped in the divine presence. That presence is something we cannot see, feel, hear, or touch, yet it is fully present in everything we can.

As I reflect on the question of God, I remember the barn in our backyard and the chickens that lived there. Sometimes when I collected eggs for our mother's table, I would feel a little chick pecking inside the egg shell. It was as if that chick had exhausted the available nourishment and felt motivated to discover new resources for its journey. Time to be born into a new world!

Or think of a tiny fly riding for its whole short life on the back of an elephant. Suddenly that fly overcomes its inertia and flies off the elephant. When it looks back, it sees the elephant for the first time with a fresh perspective—much like the early astronauts who looked back and saw the Earth as a blue-green bulb, hanging like a Christmas ornament in the deep dark cosmos.

As we continue our journey, we realize that mystery is God's other name. As we simultaneously explore our own interiority and the vast cosmos, we experience the living God as a mysterious burst of awe and wonder. It is only as we rest in the unknown yet felt sense of the sacred that we dare to discover meaning and purpose in our lives.

Everything Is Holy

Everything is holy.
Sand, stars and sea,
everything is holy.

Love, friendship and grace,
everything is holy.

How to respond
to so much abundance,
goodness, possibility and hope?

Now is the time to see
through every ray of sunshine,
every drop of dew,
everything is holy.

Speak to me
of what I do not know,
tales I long for in my heart.

Tell me stories
of everything
that today is holy.

Engaged Mystics

This new understanding of the place we humans fill in the web of life requires that we become engaged mystics. Mysticism is a unitive experience. One of the things about past religious practices is that they've often taught us morality without mysticism. We've been told what rules to keep but have not been encouraged to experience the divine in order to energize and nourish our souls. Without such experiences, we lack the moral courage and critical consciousness that will empower us to do justice. Justice-making without mysticism becomes plodding. It's obligation without celebration.

Mysticism is nourished by creation. If we were living on a lunar landscape, our souls would shrink, our spirituality would be diminished. The mystical tradition will nourish us for the journey we have ahead. It is an unmediated relationship with God. It can happen in your room, it can happen in the park, it can happen in your kitchen, it can happen in your encounter with your spouse or children, it can happen in a personal way.

The mystics talk about the notion of breakthrough. Breakthrough doesn't mean that God wasn't there before and when you have a breakthrough, God shows up. Rather, it means that you are open to the divine presence in a new way. This awareness of the divine presence is in no way a reason not to work for justice and the eradication of poverty.

Aujourd'hui Liberté

Aujourd'hui
sing a song of praise
to the wonderous One.
Gaze deeply into
the bottomless abyss
and breathe
a prayer of thanks.

On this amazing day,
celebrate the gift of life.
Under no circumstance
and for no reason,
can be it be taken away
or extinguished
on this liberté day.

New Things

I will rise
in the beauty of an ancestor,
affection of a keepsake,
loss of a dream.

Now is a new time,
infused with moments
of vision and much pain,
the joy of the unexpected.

Mystery heals all longing,
returns to us
abundance and new life.

The Ancient One Appears

What do I hear as I listen
to the empty silence
and the chatter
in the backroom of my soul?

Perhaps a voice of adoration
praising flowers in the field,
chanting from the pond,
a chorus in the night.

"Listen, listen,"
I hear my heart say.
"There is much wisdom here.
Listen, listen, the ancient one appears.

God is a Verb

Each day when we reflect on the gift of beauty manifest in the natural world, we arrive at a new emergent meaning for our planetary home.

With an indigenous mind, we are able to explore the root cause of species loss, the diminishment of topsoil, and the vast devastation taking place on our planet.

Thomas Berry offers wise advice: "The universe is a communion of subjects rather than a collection of objects." Herein lies an insight into the devastation of our planet: in some indigenous languages, communication is primarily through verbs. Nouns exist as forms of a verb. In some Native American cultures, God is a verb.

In contrast, Western languages communicate mainly through nouns. This use of nouns encourages the perception of oneself as the subject and of an "other" as the object, rather than allowing the perception of everything as one flow of action.

I believe we can all learn from the indigenous mind and the way it communes with the natural world, the way it celebrates divine presence and listens to the Earth speak. I invite you to try it. Can you see all of life through the lens of a verb?

Blessed Be

The world before us
is amazing, delicate,
luscious and wounded.
Let this magnificent paradox
heal you and every tender thing
that arises from within,
immersed and soaked
in all that is sacred.

May each eager soul
find comfort.
May each new moment
overflow with peace.
May each anxious day
bask in wisdom
and new life.
Dare to shout to all,
"Blessed be!
Blessed be!"

Moments of Sacredness and Depth

Deep within the heart of the universe there is a profound inclination to commune, to be at one with, to heal the great emptiness and abyss that reside in the enduring desire for relationship and oneness. Relationships receive their vitality from within the recesses that reside at the edge of the soul, life, Earth, and the divine origins of all that is.

Within these levels of existence lives the pulsating presence of the divine, a presence that hovers over all creation and permeates each particle. This presence evokes the wonder and awe that activate the spontaneity of the soul. As we follow the relentless invitation to create a new culture out of the fusion of cosmic consciousness and social forms, we discover our identity in relationship to each other, the planet, and our God.

A Silent Call

Where can I go
but to the way of nothingness,
that empty place from which
unplanned intuition is born.

Yes, from apparent nothingness
the unimaginable bursts forth.
What was not before comes to be.
From mystery,
an unbidden voice calls out.

Out of wonder,
the beauty of new life appears.
Peace and wonder fill the world.
Amen. Alleluia. Amen.

Thoughts on Death

A three-year-old child waves out the window of an airplane, "Hi, Daddy!" He then turns to his mother and announces confidently, "My daddy is an angel. I'm talking to him!" He is the son of the professional football player who died suddenly on the practice field.

An elder was asked, "Where are you going to go when you die?" His wise response was, "I'm not going anywhere."

These two incidents fly in the face of the conventional wisdom that says, "When you are dead, you're gone and you either go up (heaven) or down (the other place)." You certainly don't stay here.

Death is an even greater mystery than illustrated by these examples. It seems ominous and foreboding because our dominant culture is in deep denial that it even exists. Witness how we as a society participate in "the high cost of dying" with expensive caskets, prolonged wakes, and cosmetics that elicit such responses as "Doesn't he look natural?"

It is also true that we live in a culture of death, a world where violence permeates the planet.

Yet for many, death remains a mystery, often feared and too little understood. Perhaps you have memories from your childhood when a pet died or a recollection from an Ash Wednesday ritual when you were reminded, "Remember you are dust and unto dust you will return"—experiences that only increased your confusion.

I suggest that the new story has much to teach us. We are reminded that death is integral to existence. The cycles of the seasons, the way the seed dies so that a plant may grow, are powerful proclamations that deepen our comprehension of the mystery. From the perspective of the universe, death is a next chapter in your journey, a story of returning to your origins. It is a new chapter in your life, a transformational moment on the journey.

A friend illustrated this interconnectedness of death and rebirth when she said, "I was with my father when he died and my sister when she gave birth, and the two experiences were mysteriously the same."

The story of death is that life is changed, not ended. This lesson has been revealed to us from the beginning. Through cosmological death, the galaxies were born. Earth came into being and life flourished. From the perspective of the new story, death becomes a transformative moment when we are born into a new life; a mysterious transition into a new state of existence; a communion with the divine, whereby we join the great cycle of existence.

In this view, the angel in a child's mind and the elder's claim for his continuing presence make sense. Rather than an ominous ending to be feared, death becomes a threshold to new life, a threshold to resurrection.

Jim Conlon

Everything

I know today
what I never knew before—
that everything,
yes everything,
every child, pollywog and tree,
is pulsating with goodness.
Every child, pollywog and tree
is a sacrament,
a messenger to the world.

Awaken, dear friend,
this is what I trust is true.
The sacred one is everywhere,
here where you are,
here where each child,
each creature of the sea
each runner of the woods,
each wonderous moment is.

Prayer to the Invisible One

Who is God?
I mean the one
who is invisible,
yet fully alive.

A rainbow
of every living thing
hovers in the far-off sky.
Do you feel
the sacred one now,
wrapped in beauty,
snuggling with you
in a blanket of peace?

Are you not the One
I cannot see,
that river of grace
that trickles through my soul
and declares,
"I am earth,
I am alive,
I am beauty,
I am wonder,
I am the hunger in your heart,
the foundation of all that is"?

The Master Narrative of the West

The Genesis story of the Hebrew Bible is the master narrative of the West. Its drama of loss and return to the garden has a profound influence on our psyches, our culture, and our way of life.

We change farms into gardens, irrigate deserts more suitable for cactus to grow lawns. Our urge is driven by a desire to get back to the garden. Theology has been shaped by this urge. Acts of acquisition and greed have been sanctioned as spiritual practices to enable us to get back to the garden.

A further extension is the doctrine popularly portrayed on bumper stickers as "He who dies with the most toys wins." We also know there is no correlation between the acquisition of wealth and possessions, and living a full and satisfied life.

We need a new story, a new Genesis: a story that is dynamic, interactive, and relational; a story that dissolves anthropocentrism, individualism, and greed; a story to enhance the work of partnership and justice; a story to nurture restoration and collaboration, which will focus our destiny, enliven our heart and be attentive to the voices of creation, liberation, and contemplation.

A Blessing

Blessed is Earth;
it shall flourish with radiant beauty.

Blessed are the waters;
they will flow with clarity
and quench our thirst.

Blessed are the trees;
they shall absorb toxins
and give us breath.

Blessed are the birds;
they shall soar stately in the sky.

Blessed are those in pain;
they shall discover radiance in the dark.

Blessed are those who despair;
they shall be enveloped in hopeful peace.

Blessed is the fire;
it shall melt all walls and separation
with the energies of love.

Blessed are they
who live in the universe,
who are inclusive of all,
who celebrate the resacralization of the planet,
for they shall experience beauty
in all that is revealed.

Revisioning Roots

I return again and again to this question: "What is it that I believe?" We can rephrase this question as "What do I trust?" "Trust" is a better word than "believe" because belief is cognitive, while trust is affective.

For each of us, there is a core conviction that grounds us, that is visceral and that is rooted in certainty. One of the challenges in dealing with our tradition is that sometimes our core convictions seem at odds with our inherited tradition. The result is that we feel stifled and stuck.

Through reflection, we can discover an alignment between the truth that is revealed in our hearts and what we have learned from our inherited traditions. It is a search for congruence. If we go deep enough into our own psychic passageways and deep enough into our tradition, we will meet the underground river that is the divine.

Bring Love and Healing to the World

From all forms of abuse,
deliver us, O Lord.

From violence and discrimination,
deliver us, O Lord.

From pain and desperation,
deliver us, O Lord.

From poverty and neglect,
deliver us, O Lord.

From rejection and despair,
deliver us, O Lord.

From the chains of incarceration,
deliver us, O Lord.

From suffering and misery,
deliver us, O Lord.

From injustice and exploitation,
deliver us, O Lord.

From loneliness and rejection
deliver us, O Lord.

For recovery and celebration,
we give great thanks, O Lord.

Jim Conlon

For loving moments of the heart,
we give great thanks, O Lord.

For the care and protection
of our common home
we give great thanks, O Lord.

Up Ahead

Arise, my friends,
from the dark forest
trembling in the night,
the waning moon above.

This is the night
where only God can see,
in this darkest opaque hour,
an iridescent spark.

We are reminded
at this transfiguration moment
to be like Abraham of old,
to sacrifice our objects for the world.

Only as people willing to surrender
what we hold most precious
can we find that most marvelous gift
waiting up ahead.

Engaged Spirituality: Pathways to Wisdom

At this moment of destruction and decline, we search for a new identity and ability to act. When we become consciously attuned to the dynamics of the universe and act in alignment with this awareness, we have begun to discover an engaged spirituality.

The hunger for sacredness and depth resides in soul, life, and Earth. This hunger is healed, responded to, and nourished by an experience of the divine as we participate in a mystical and engaged spirituality.

In an engaged spirituality, we awaken to the creative energy that streams through the cosmos. We understand that our role is to give this energy focus and expression. We fulfill our destiny and participate in the transformation of a broken world when we engage in this work.

Engaged spirituality draws on a wisdom that is both ancient and new. From the deep wells of tradition, we gain access to the wisdom that resides in the recesses of the universe and our souls.

Through engaged spirituality, we penetrate the profound mysteries embedded in existence and made palpably present through symbol, myth, and analogy.

Engaged spirituality is an immersion into the creative

powers of the universe and the most direct contact a human can have with the divine.

Engaged spirituality reveals new insights into the great cultural workers of the past and present, as we view their practice through the lens of the universe.

Engaged spirituality enhances our ability to act. We become aware that the creative energy of the universe is pulsating through our lives and activating every aspect of our being.

Engaged spirituality nurtures a critical reflection that gives expression to a cosmic longing that calls us to heal what is broken and transform the face of the Earth, as we strive to make all things new.

Engaged spirituality is a new context for our journey, a place where poet and politician are one, a cosmic journey of struggle and fulfillment.

Engaged spirituality is a means to embrace intimacy and contemplation, communion and solitude, inwardness and prophetic action, impulse and practice, mystery and engagement, cultural work and cosmic consciousness.

Engaged spirituality activates the imagination and reminds us of our kinship with all life and the beauty present in each relationship.

Engaged spirituality invites us to discover the membranes of meaning present in each new moment, to perceive each encounter as a threshold to sacredness.

Engaged spirituality invites us to align our energies with the dynamics of an unfolding universe and to accomplish whatever needs to be done to nurture compassion and new life

Engaged spirituality creates a context for fresh pathways to wisdom that are mystical, poetic, and profoundly interrelated.

Engaged spirituality empowers us to accomplish whatever needs to be done and to make it possible for depth, freedom, beauty, and compassion to shine forth.

Through engaged spirituality, we participate in meaningful action that is congruent with our worldviews, true to our vision of the future, aligned with the unfolding of our lives, and transformative for the entire community of life.

Engaged spirituality challenges us to transform our consciousness and our conscience. We are invited to weave together webs of wisdom and programs of action. As we honor the aspirations of the heart, we rediscover the God of the universe, and set our sails toward a hope-filled future.

I identified the following themes of engaged spirituality.

Magnanimity and the liberation of creation. Engagement in deep cultural work nourishes a magnanimity of spirit. In the process, we experience a felt-sense of oneness with the universe and all that is. Our engagement inspires a deep communion with humanity and the other-than-human world. We transcend narrow self-interest and are moved to grant each member of the Earth community the freedom to inhabit the planet and fulfill its role. We are inspired by the generosity demonstrated by the self-giving of the sun.

Originating energy and the sacred impulse. The process of transformation finds its direction and energy in responding to the felt-sense of a sacred impulse that prompts our action, an impulse we understand as the continuing expression of the originating energy that gave birth to the universe and continues to support our efforts and intuition.

Cosmic dynamics and geo-justice. The harmony, balance, and peace embedded in the universe find their cultural manifestation in the work of geo-justice. In this process, beauty shines forth and divinity becomes palpable in our midst as we celebrate communion (global), differentiation (local) and interiority (psycho-social) in cultural form.

Consciousness and culture. Engaged spirituality is an irreversible process that weaves together our cultural work with an awareness of the unfolding universe. We experience the support and interaction of consciousness and conscience. Our cosmological consciousness and our awareness of the world community create an integral presence. The result is that we act in accordance with what we see, and our cultural work evolves and unfolds within the evolving universe.

Creation, destruction and the dynamics of rebirth. Cultural work involves the capacity to die to oneself and rise to the concern for the other. These deep dynamics of creation, destruction, and rebirth are embedded in the process of life and in the dynamics of our traditions. They find expression in the epiphanies (incarnation), Gethsemane moments (cross), and inevitable outpouring of new life in the larger arc of existence (resurrection).

The heart, listening to the universe. Deep listening is a practice that resonates in the recesses of the cultural worker. It is understood as an echo from the pulsating heart of the universe. Listening to the other and to the heart of the universe creates a fabric of meaning and wisdom and fosters new moments of mutuality for Earth and every species.

Roots of engagement. An engaged spirituality will be rooted in a felt-sense of interdependence (contemplation), a desire that all peoples be free (liberation), and a reverence for a resacralized Earth (creation).

Interrelatedness and communion. Our work is nourished and energized by inseparability and the desire to commune with all members of the "Noah's Ark of Existence." We are drawn forth by longing to make belonging in the universe possible and to dissolve the separation, exile, alienation, and loneliness that prevent authentic relationships with soul, life, Earth and the divine.

Creatine energy and the celebration of uniqueness. The universe mirrors the divine act of creativity and participates in abundant acts of creativity and expressions of new life. Each person dances into the future, with a unique capacity for creativity and celebration of new life.

Only Good Survives

Where the exaltation of accomplishment
matches the agony of defeat,
raise your hopes on high,
settle for nothing but your best.

You are the vibrant fusion
that intersects
joy and sorrow
and everything in between.

Now is the moment
to plunge into this wild, empty place,
where nothing disappears
and everything remains.

Here among the untamed,
the untethered and unseen,
only good survives,
yes, only good survives.

God's Work in this World

In the gospel, we find Mary and Joseph seeking for their son, who reminds them he must be about his Father's business.

When we think about what we must do to be about our Father's business—to do God's work in this world—we can perhaps receive encouragement and guidance from Thomas Merton. He proposed that our vocation and calling in life are to pray ourselves into the future and to work together with God to create our own life, our own identity and purpose.

We can learn from the moment Thomas experienced liberation from the confinement of his skin-encapsulated ego and entered the ocean of grace. In this epiphany, he discovered that the dazzling light in his soul was the same dazzling light that ignited the origin of the universe.

When we become our true self and awaken from the dream of separateness, we realize anew that we can do God's work in this world.

May Conflict Subside

Tumult across the land,
anger and division
rule the day,
here on our endangered home.

Toxic terror
penetrates my soul,
yet in the chaos and confusion,
I see the face of God.

May the danger recede,
bring peace across the land.
Now is the time, my friends;
may our prayer come true.

With each passing day,
I sense planetary peace
across a new horizon,
and welcome what is yet to be.

From Turbulence to Transformation

The journey of a soul in a time of transition can feel like a ride down a turbulent river. The rapids of crisis and change are often precarious. In the upheaval, the soul is sometimes submerged, gasping for air, swirling out of control. Yet when we can let go and trust the deepest current of life, we find that even in the most chaotic waters of change there is always a buoyancy, and the water is ever fertile with the promise of birth. Personal crises ever hold the possibility of passage to a new level of maturity, to a deeper, more compassionate ground of living. Successfully navigating these turbulent waters of transition requires accessing the wisdom of the past and preparing to meet the challenges of the future, while responding fully and creatively to the present moment of grace held within the crisis.

What is true of personal times of transition is also true in social and communal crises. Within each turbulent eddy of crisis there is a still point of grace, a point for pondering the divine presence and gathering our resources to stay afloat. In this still point, we realize that we are not alone as we ride the rapids of change and transition. We realize that we can form networks that are vehicles for relationship as well as interconnecting webs that keep us afloat.

We come together to discover our allies, identify our strengths, explore our potential for growth, review our vision, and develop strategies for coping with the changes taking place. We realize we are not just being taken for a ride but can actually affect the course of our journey. When we come together and are provided with information and support, we listen to one another's voices, reflect on our inner promptings, and adjust our course. This process enables us to look toward the future with hope—a future that will be realized from within the ever-expanding constellation of relationships and support.

In the still point, we become aware not only of our mutual support but of the Spirit that sustains us and provides us a vision of the possible to impel us on our journey. In this divine buoyancy, we realize that accomplishing the work of transition requires tolerance for turbulence and uncertainty. This important capacity is accompanied by a radical trust that balance and direction will come out of what appears to be chaos. From this place of ambiguity and emerging order, we continue Christ's work of shaping a shared destiny of planetary liberation and profound fulfillment, a process referred to as the coming of God's reign. For this work of transition only can be accomplished when it is nourished by an intimate experience of the divine. Only when our individual and corporate efforts are grounded in God can we summon the necessary courage and strength to achieve what often appears overwhelming and impossible: the great work of realizing the historical mission of humanity as we welcome and usher in the age of justice, peace, and the integrity of creation.

This new worldview and the strategies and tactics that accompany its application are born out of the collective imaginations of scientists, artists, theologians, and activists. When they—and all of us together—listen and respond to divine revelation as it is expressed in traditional ways, as well as throughout creation and within the human spirit, these new understandings will extend into the area of cultural transformation. As we listen to the voiceless of the Earth, we take up the enormous challenges of restructuring education, religion, and public and corporate life with the goal of ushering Earth and all its peoples into an era of harmony and peace. This fresh and anticipated moment promises to be personally enriching and beneficial for all creation.

To function in this new era will require decisive and collaborative action; the magnitude of the task will require a community of creative and dedicated people whose diverse backgrounds and gifts will be brought into focus by a transcendent and common goal.

As we engage in change, we realize that each moment of transition evokes memories of gratitude for what has gone before, for all we have received. Simultaneously, the waters of transition invite us to embrace the future. During this daring and delicate time of moving into an unknown future, the process of those engaged in this great adventure will be spirited, participatory, and hopeful. A focus on the future will empower us to withstand the predictable tidal waves of resistance in the forms of accusation, innuendo, and half-truths. Such turbulence ever calls us to return to the still point of grace, wherein we engage in the quest for the divine and the struggle to transcend ego involvement and self-delusion. It is here in the fertile womb of silence that new vision is born, that we will discover our place and path in the larger drama of life.

The entire process of the soul in a time of such transition is focused and stabilized through connecting with trusted colleagues and doing everything possible to capture each precious moment as an opportunity to ignite a new consciousness, a new ethos, and a new culture.

At all times on the immense journey toward a new understanding of the drama of our origins and destiny we will be energized by gratitude and freed by a capacity to surrender any impulse to dominate or control. Only then will the divine plan reveal itself in mysterious and powerful ways; only then will those engaged in the journey of transition be able to access the capacity to endure this profound period of growth, decline, and renewal. Only then will we be energized to move into the future from a context of radical reciprocity based on an affirmation of core values and commitments previously made.

Involvement in this prophetic effort will stretch the envelope of our imagination regarding what is possible and will thrust us into a future where there is full congruence between authority and self-initiative, vision and practice, lifestyle and engaged spirituality, personal integrity and professional responsibility. Always there will be an allegiance to a well-developed strategy to invent and execute programs in which leadership demonstrates a healthy disregard for status or stature. To accomplish this task, each person must place performance over ego, continuity over chaos, trust over suspicion, gratitude over greed. Only in this way will it be possible to design and develop the delicate and prophetic vehicle so necessary and needed to usher in a new era. The values and vehicles for the task have never been more needed.

The emerging goal of our journey will become ever more constant and clear: to liberate ourselves and all involved from personal oppression and the structures of domination. Inspired by a glimpse of newfound freedom and aroused by the struggle for fulfillment on a personal and cultural level, each of us will embrace this new moment of grace with rigorous effort and an engaged spiritual practice.

Strengthened by mental discipline and a willingness to embrace the magnitude of the task, convinced that each of us and our collective efforts are indeed "bathed in God," we move forward fully prepared to exercise the courage to create a vital constellation of functional relationships. From here, each one will take up the challenge that is based on truth, conscious of the past and predicated on the vision of an enchanting future.

The Spirit Speaks

Words well up.
They speak for themselves
of many things,
of sacred turbulence,
of wonder and surprise,
of awesome beauty,
and the deepest aspirations of the heart.

Beauty beckons us
to suffer and rejoice,
to allow the paradox of presence
to engage us all,
and from agony and ecstasy,
to see uniqueness born.

This is my surprise for you.
This is my true joy,
that beauty will be born
and that all you hope for
will make you free.

Toward a Viable Future

Our journey toward a healthy, functional future requires an openness to new states of consciousness, to welcoming the unexpected in our lives—whether insights, actions, or relationships. We are invited to consider the impact of a new vision for life that sees all of creation functioning in an interrelated, mutually enhancing, and interdependent way. This perspective sheds light on our place in the unfolding drama of the universe. It is a worldview that generates gratitude and fresh psychic energy for the challenges that lie ahead. We can understand this energy as a fire that burns deeply, with passion and compassion, to heal the wounds of the human and other-than-human world. This energy evokes within us a new mysticism that can become a crucible for a life charged with beauty, vision, and divine presence. We will be enriched when we explore the longing that penetrates our souls, our lives, our planet, and the divine.

It is commonly understood that crises can provide opportunity for change and assist us to move forward in new and unprecedented ways, to see things differently, and subsequently to act differently. As we look back upon the rubble of a post-industrial age, we begin to see what we have done and perhaps ask why we are here and what we are called to do in the face of a dangerous yet hopeful future. The crisis invites us to engage in the work of transformation and become people with listening hearts. This work will nurture a renewed sensitivity and our capacity to take up the challenge of healing the tragedy we have caused.

We will extend our awareness and compassion beyond the human, and generously respond to this particular moment of grace and opportunity for transformation. With a renewed sense of awe and wonder, we work to transform the dominant cultural paradigm.

Your Questions Know

How do I tell you
about mystery,
share with you
those precious things
I still do not know?

The chickadee could tell you,
I am confident,
also a raven and a cat.

My words get in the way.
The soul knows
what I as yet cannot tell.

Gaze into mystery
and let your questions
tell it all.

Resurgamus

Shortly before his life was taken by an assassin's bullet, Archbishop Oscar Romero proclaimed to his people, "If they kill me, I will rise in the people of El Salvador."

It was true, as his picture became visible in every classroom home and chapel across that small country of Central America torn asunder by violence and war.

I recall the time—which seems like yesterday, but was years ago—when I visited a mudslide on a hillside in El Salvador where many people were buried. Painted across the hillside in large letters was "Resurgamus," or "we will rise again," another testimony to their indomitable spirit.

Longing and Belonging

Each of the classical traditions points us to a place of ultimate belonging: nirvana, heaven, paradise. Each of these represents a state of mystical union. Realized eschatology is a theological term for letting heaven happen now, for making the future present in our midst in this moment.

Science reveals that we live in a web of relationship, and that the cosmos itself is a place of belonging. This web of relationship is a pattern that connects us all. Belonging can heal the despair that stalks our culture and diminishes hope. When hope springs up in the soul, we become connected with life, with Earth, and the divine.

There is a connection between longing, belonging, and chaos. The absence of belonging is longing. When we're in a state of longing, we're off balance because we're reaching for something—for a connection, a relationship; something to ground us, to root us. This chaotic state is uncomfortable yet essential for change. The chaotic state is really the precursor of something opening up that can take us to another level, another place, another journey. Chaos is often the threshold to belonging.

The longing we experience is the capacity to deal with internal dislocation and the uncertainty about our traditions, our communities, and our lives. This uncertainty can be the energetic force that moves us to a new state of coherence. Change won't happen without dislocation:

cultural dislocation, intrapsychic dislocation, relational dislocation.

This new territory is often disturbing, dangerous, and challenging. It is also refreshing, inviting, and new. The capacity to embrace the instability of our existence—to hold it in community with friends, in our meditative reflective times, in our bodies, in our traditions, and in our prayer—gives us the capacity to belong in new ways. This movement toward belonging is beginning to happen.

David Bohm is famous for saying, "There is no scientific evidence for separation." There's a lot of sociological and cultural evidence, but there's no scientific evidence. If we can meditate on belonging in the universe, we will experience belonging. Everything belongs. All of us belong. The trees belong. The puppies belong. The worms belong. The rain belongs. Everything is related and interconnected.

Consider the following situations. Where did you feel you didn't belong?

- Have you ever been in a country where you felt you didn't belong?

- Have you had an experience where you felt you didn't belong because of your ethnicity, religion, gender, or race?

- Have you ever felt rooted in your own tradition, yet felt you did not belong in that tradition?

- Have you ever been confronted with a political situation where you felt alienated or at odds with those in power?

Now consider times when you did belong:

- Have you ever felt a sense of belonging through friendship?

- Have you ever felt a connection with the divine, God, source, spirit? Have you ever felt you belonged to God?

- Have you ever felt you belonged in your family, community, or other group?

- Have you ever felt that you belonged to a sense of destiny about your existence?

- Where have you felt most that you belonged?

Images of Tomorrow

As we stand at the edge of wonder, positioned at the threshold of sacredness, images of tomorrow emerge into consciousness, bringing a new vision of hope to a world immersed in anxiety.

We draw hope from a new vision of monastery, whose architecture is created out of the dynamic relationships that are nurtured by the wonder of the universe and our place in the future.

We draw hope from a fresh vision of a novitiate, whereby each person's cosmological imagination reveals what it means to be human in an unfolding universe.

We draw hope from a renewed sense of home, an experience whereby we are reenergized to heal the wound of homelessness, and we become energized for the journey, like a horse who enthusiastically gallops when pointed toward home.

We draw hope from a gallery of beauty that touches every soul and reminds us of the gorgeous planet that invites us to commune and be at one.

Imagine planting a small oak tree. You may not be there when that little sapling becomes a tall oak. Yet, without the initial planting, watering, and care, there will be no tall oak. The work of engaged spirituality is like planting trees to keep alive a hope-filled promise of a better tomorrow. Each of us is like a tree of life, with our roots placed deeply in the earth, giving birth to a new economic system of sustainability and diversity. The trunk is a biocracy and a fully functioning democracy. The branches are a meta-religious movement that supports, nurtures, and motivates all initiatives toward a more mutually enhancing relationship with Earth. The leaves represent the wisdom of all traditions, and a deepening commitment to a preferential option for the Earth.

Beatitudes for an Engaged Spirituality

Blessed are the hopeful:
they hold a promise of tomorrow.

Blessed are the courageous:
they embrace the challenge of today.

Blessed are the forgiving:
they are free of the burden of the past.

Blessed are people of prolonged engagement:
they will create a better world for the children.

Blessed are the disappointed:
they will rise and anticipate a better day.

Blessed are the self-forgetful:
they will engage in a compassionate embrace.

Blessed are the flowers
bursting forth in the spring:
they will bring beauty to the Earth.

Blessed are the children:
they will celebrate spontaneity and new life.

Blessed are the contemplatives:
they will embrace the universe as one.

Blessed are the liberators:
they will set all the captives free.

Blessed are the engaged mystics:
they will ignite afire on the Earth
and unite the stars with the street.

Our New Threshold Moment

This is and can be a second Genesis, a threshold in time, a defining moment, a new beginning. It is time for a new Exodus as well: a moment to liberate our worldviews, cultural work, and spiritual practice from the confinement of conformity and outmoded approaches. An engaged spirituality will embrace both the ancient and new, cultural and cosmic, in order to heal our endangered planet and declining culture.

As we look to the future, in a sense, we turn toward home. As Thomas Berry would say, it's like "riding a horse and buggy" and turning toward home. When we feel the horse drawn toward its destination, a fresh energy empowers its journey and we move at a more rapid and enthusiastic pace.

Such a turning will be a second Exodus, a time like that of the Copernican Revolution, when humanity was freed of the illusion that the Earth was the center of the universe and everything revolved around it. This second Exodus will require new myths and stories—a new master narrative; a new geography of soul, life, Earth, and the divine.

The new life that will emerge among us will be marked by the birth of a new meta-religious understanding, a new perception of the divine, a new politics and economics, and a new meaning of peace.

This new transformation will be a rebirth that will call on and access both the creative and collective energy of the past, as well as the fresh visions and dreams being born in the hearts and minds of people today. A new meaning of love will be nurtured in the embrace of all those relationships that hold us together in this new world, this new web of life.

Engagement and the Divine:
Action/Reflection

How has a deepened awareness of the emergent universe prepared you to participate in an engaged spirituality?

In light of a new understanding, what are your primary areas of concern for our planet at the threshold of a new era?

What actions do you plan to undertake to bring peace, joy, and compassion to our world and every species?

Rediscovering the Divine

We rediscover the divine as we:

- Engage in collaborative projects that are marked by reciprocity, mutuality, and a new level of community

- Support personal and planetary challenges that are holistic and visionary, leading to passionate and practical action to bring balance to relationships and liberation to Earth and every species

- Explore lifestyles that are increasingly congruent with the dynamics of the universe; that enhance an integral human presence; and that are born out of awe, wisdom, and radical amazement

- Discover and develop ways to engage in meaningful and collaborative action that is aligned to our world-view and vision of the future

- Ponder deeply key questions that connect the heart of humanity to the heart of the cosmos, to renew and inspire the soul at this threatening moment in our history

- Celebrate the intuitions that ignite our imaginations and summon us to engage in a spiritual journey grounded in our origins and marked by the touchstone categories of reciprocity, information, support, and common action

- Journey to the edge of our longing and heal our hunger for sacredness and depth as we create together a planetary community that is enveloped in courage, spontaneity, and aspirations for good work

About the Author

Jim Conlon was born in Canada in 1936. He received a degree in chemsity from Assumption University of Windsor, and later in theology from the University of Western Ontario, and a PhD from Union Institute and Graduate School. Deeply moved by the impact of the second Vatican Council, the civil rights movement, and the Vietnam War, Jim moved from pastoral work to the streets. Today he is one of the leading teachers of the new narrative of the cosmos. Visit him online at www.jimconlon.net and on Facebook at www.facebook.com/becomingplanetarypeople.

Also Available from Jim Conlon

Becoming Planetary People: 978-0-9964387-0-4

Geo-Justice: 978-0-9964387-2-8

Wondering Between Two Worlds: 978-0-692-08364-2

CPSIA information can be obtained
at www.ICGtesting.com
Printed in the USA
BVHW042009240319
543559BV00005B/14/P

9 780578 403731